What passing-bells for these who died as cattle?
Only the monstrous anger of the guns.
Only the stuttering rifles' rapid rattle
Can patter out their hasty orisons.

DIEPPE, DIEPPE

BRERETON GREENHOUS

DIEPPE, DIEPPE

ART GLOBAL

Canadian Cataloguing in Publication Data

Greenhous, Brereton, 1929-
    Dieppe, Dieppe
    Includes bibliographical references.
    ISBN 2-920718-52-5
1. Dieppe, Raid, 1942. 2. World War, 1939-1945 —
Naval operations, Canadian. 3. World War, 1939-1945 —
Naval operations, British. I. Title.
D756.5.D5G73 1993   940.54'21425   C93-096788-7

Project Coordinator: Serge Bernier

Endpaper:
Jean Paul Lemieux (1904-1990)
Soldat, 1982
Oil on canvas, 41 cm x 51.1 cm
Private collection, Quebec
Photograph by Jean-Guy Kérouac
Epigraph by Wilfred Owen
from his poem
Anthem for Doomed Youth

Jacket illustration by Stéphane Geoffrion from
Jean Paul Lemieux's painting, *Soldat*

Design and Production:
Art Global, Montreal

Printed and bound in Canada

Cet ouvrage a été publié simultanément en français sous le titre de:
Dieppe, Dieppe
ISBN 2-920718-53-3

Published by Éditions Art Global Inc.
in cooperation with the Department of National Defence
and under license from the
Canada Communication Group — Publishing, Supply and Services Canada.

ISBN 2-920718-52-5 (Art Global)

ACKNOWLEDGEMENTS

The comments of the Director-General History, Department of National Defence, Alec Douglas, improved this manuscript substantially, as did the suggestions and material help of my colleagues at DGHist, Roger Sarty, Stephen Harris, Michael Whitby, Don Graves, Bob Caldwell and Richard Gimblett. The maps were supplied by William Constable, and Serge Bernier bore the administrative and co-ordinating burdens of the project.

My thanks are also due to Brian Villa of the University of Ottawa for his enthusiastic support and criticisms. At the National Archives of Canada, Tim Dubé, Ernie Butler, Michel Wyczynski and Micheline Robert were most kind in uncovering accounts of JUBILEE and supplying photographs of training for RUTTER. In London, England, Jane Sampson turned up relevant material at the Public Record Office and selected photographs from the Imperial War Museum.

However, all judgements and interpretations (and, of course, any errors of fact) are entirely the author's responsibility.

INTRODUCTION

Dieppe, Dieppe... In Canadian ears the word resounds with all the ritual solemnity of a funeral bell. 'Life, struck sharp on death, makes awful lightning,' wrote Elizabeth Barrett Browning, and in our national memory Operation JUBILEE has made such awful lightning that fact is sometimes hard to separate from fiction.

Some facts are all too clear, however. Four thousand, nine hundred and sixty-three Canadian soldiers embarked for Dieppe on 18 August 1942. The next day 907 of them, or better than 18 percent, were either killed on the beaches in some 11 horrifying hours, or subsequently died of wounds, or died in enemy hands. Another 2,460, or nearly 50 percent, were wounded, and the 1,874 taken prisoner included 568 of those wounded. Only 336 of the 2,210 who returned to England (between two and three hundred of whom had not even landed) got back unharmed.

More Canadian casualties had been incurred in less time on three occasions during the First World War — at Vimy and Passchendaele and Amiens — but those great battles were accounted victories and, as percentages, the losses were not nearly so great. Sometimes smaller groups suffered severely in percentage terms, in either victory or defeat — but in those cases the absolute numbers involved were too slight to make a national impact.

'The only thing more melancholy than a battle won,' observed the Duke of Wellington after winning at Waterloo, away back in 1814, 'is a battle lost.' At Hong Kong, in December 1941 — like Dieppe, a battle lost — 290 Canadians had been killed or died of wounds in a week of fighting, 14.7 per cent of the 1,973 who had left Canada a month earlier. One hundred and thirty-two more died in harrowing captivity over the next three and a half years.

The overall death rate from Hong Kong was 21.3 per cent, a figure greater than that from Dieppe but one nevertheless ameliorated by time and scale, so that the attention paid to it by Canadian historians has been correspondingly slight. Dieppe, on the other hand, combined a higher percentage of actual battle casualties with significantly larger numbers, all during a very brief span of time, to make an indelible mark; and, happily, nothing that happened after it — Ortona, the Liri Valley, Verrières Ridge, Woensdrecht, the Hochwald — has matched that malignant combination.

Over the years, a veritable flood of words has been written on JUBILEE. At least thirty books or pamphlets in English or French (and one in German) have the raid as a primary focus; all the relevant regimental histories make much of it; and there have been half a dozen television documentaries or docu-dramas, two stage plays, an epic poem, and innumerable articles in books, journals and newspapers on the subject.

The first coherent account (despite his tendency to downplay inept planning and accept too readily the easy excuses of senior officers), came from the pen of the Canadian Army's official historian, Colonel C.P. Stacey, in *Six Years of War* (1955). He made it clear that the convolutions and contradictions of planning and preparation would not be easy to follow. Although it was 'in general a very well documented operation,' he affirmed (with considerable exaggeration) that 'the documentation with reference to its *origins and objects* — points of special importance — [was] far from complete' [his emphasis].

He might have added, but did not, that key evidence concerning its implementation was also often lacking. With so much dependent on surprise secrecy was paramount beforehand, and afterwards ego and ambition brought more concealment. Some evidence would seem to have been carefully suppressed by the Chief of Combined Operations, Lord Louis

Mountbatten, and his naval adviser, Captain John Hughes-Hallet, the eventual Naval Force commander for JUBILEE. And some was certainly destroyed by Sir Bernard Montgomery, the responsible authority for the cancelled Operation RUTTER, who deliberately burned anything that might 'incriminate' him and then lied about his part in the planning process, if his official biographer is to be believed.

The Military Force commander, Canadian Major-General John Hamilton Roberts, who was made the scapegoat for failure, chose to maintain the silence of an officer and gentleman — 'never explain, never complain' — all his life. An exemplary attitude from a soldier's perspective, it has nevertheless frustrated historians poking through the ashes of Dieppe for pieces of a bizarre puzzle.

Although they add much colour (as well as all kinds of fantasy), to Stacey's work, subsequent accounts have added little of significance, with the notable exceptions of Brian Loring Villa's prize-winning piece of revisionism, *Unauthorized Action: Mountbatten and the Dieppe Raid* (1989), John P. Campbell's all-too-brief study of 'Air Operations and the Dieppe Raid' in *Aerospace Historian* (April 1976), and J.R. Robinson's illuminating piece on 'Radar Intelligence and the Dieppe Raid' in the *Canadian Defence Quarterly* (April 1991). Günther Peis's *The Mirror of Deception* (1977) — much of which is devoted to other topics than Dieppe — considers the question of German foreknowledge, and will remain the best work in the field until we reap the benefit of John Campbell's forthcoming *Dieppe Revisited: A Documentary History*, to be published in London later this year.

There is an old adage — nonetheless true for its antiquity — that victory has many fathers but defeat is an orphan. No one was ever anxious to claim responsibility for this catastrophe; and the circumstances surrounding it were, by both accident and design, so convoluted and obscure that those who were responsible were able to 'de-personalize' the issue to a considerable extent. In doing so, they were aided over many years, by the quite brilliant public relations skills of Mountbatten, who, for the rest of his life, (ably assisted by Hughes-Hallett, who possibly had even more to hide) devoted immense amounts of time and energy to suppressing or neutralizing criticism. Nevertheless, with the opening up of both public and private archives and the painstaking work of a few good men, much more is now known about the politics and planning of RUTTER, and its re-mounting as JUBILEE, than was revealed by Stacey's pen.

At the same time, all sorts of myths and misconceptions have arisen that badly require refutation. There is no evidence that the Germans on the spot (or even in the general vicinity) had advance knowledge of the raid; or that the British prime minister and/or his chiefs of staff intended it to fail, in order to reduce Russian (or American) pressure for a Second Front. Few, if any, lessons were learned that could not have been learned just as effectively and far more cheaply by intelligent analysis of possibilities and technology and the application of common sense to properly thought-out training.

This book attempts to pull together, at a popular level and in a relatively brief fashion, the various strands of policy and personality, grand strategy, operations and tactics, by land, sea and air, that brought about the 'awful lightning' of Dieppe.

Whenever practicable the words of actual participants in these events have been used — *they are distinguished by italic type;* and (since recollections often change over the years in favour of more dramatic, amusing or self-serving versions) with the notable exception of Albert Kirby's unique memoir they are as contemporary, or near-contemporary, words as research permits.

CHAPTER I

CHAPTER I

'A COASTAL TOWN CALLED DEEPY'

That calm and lovely night of 18/19 August 1942, Able Seaman Albert Kirby was at the helm of R-135, a Landing Craft Personnel (Large), or LCP(L), to give it its formal Royal Navy nomenclature. Informally, such vessels were known as R-boats, or sometimes Higgins boats after their American designer and builder. Constructed of plywood on a steel frame, flat-bottomed, 37 feet long and 11 feet wide with a noisy gasoline engine, they were seaworthy little vessels with a good turn of speed if necessary and a cruising range of 120 miles at 9 to 11 knots.

They could, if appropriate, be lowered from the davits of a ship while fully loaded. Designed to run up on a beach bow first, they lacked any kind of a ramp, however. Anyone who wanted to get ashore in such circumstances had to scramble over the high bow, to drop four feet or more to the sand or shingle. And R-boats were certainly not bulletproof.

Kirby was the coxwain of this one, he recalled, half a century later. Beside him was the commanding officer, a sub-lieutenant of the Royal Navy; and behind them, in the well of the hull, were a petty officer mechanic, an ordinary seaman deckhand (even if there was no deck to speak of) and

36 armed men, sitting astride three hard benches that ran the length of the well.

Kirby, from Woodstock, Ontario, had volunteered for 'hazardous work' in small craft after basic training at Halifax. Since then his life had been quite extraordinarily dull. A training base in Scotland, on the banks of the Clyde, and a depot in Portsmouth were not wildly exciting places for an eighteen-year-old anxious to play his part in Hitler's downfall. He was currently serving in the 2nd Canadian Landing Craft Flotilla and thinking, *'My God, what a war! When in the world are we going to look down the barrel of a gun and see a Kraut just asking for it?'*

A week earlier, chronically short of cash, he had sold his upcoming weekend pass to a friend. Thus he had been required to substitute himself when, on the Saturday morning, his friend and two other RCN ratings had been unexpectedly called on to complete the RN crews of *'an R-boat flotilla...for a few days and then you will come right back here.'* 'But what's this Next of Kin Form all about,' [he] persisted. The R[egulating] P[etty] O[fficer] had a ready answer. 'You lads have got to ride this bloody lorry out of here, and sure as Christ made little *green apples one of you will fall out and kill yourself, and we have to know where to send your rum-soaked body.'*

When the truck reached Newhaven, Kirby was assigned to one of twenty-five R-boats that were eventually loaded with men of the Queen's Own Cameron Highlanders of Canada. On Tuesday evening the whole flotilla put to sea, for what he assumed was just one more in the endless series of exercises that had marked his naval career to date.

Darkness slowly settled on us and we eventually lost sight of all the landing craft around us. Guided only by the small blue light on the stern of R-84, we droned on relentlessly, through a night of almost tropical elegance. There was a moon, small and pale, over my right shoulder that started me thinking of home and my girlfriend in Halifax....

It is now almost 22:00 [hours = 10 p.m.] and our faithful Hall-Scott engine continues with its unrelenting roar. The moon is getting close to the horizon now, but the slow, easy ground swell of the English Channel gives us a pleasant rocking motion that I find very restful. Some of the soldiers seem to be having a hard time with the motion and look a little sick. Most are trying to get a little sleep. Our course seems to be varying between 130° and 140°. I expect the variation is being caused by the long line of landing craft slowly slithering like a snake, but in the darkness I can't see this and can only speculate. At the wheel of the craft I

am sitting here in considerable comfort, in an upholstered seat, but my heart goes out to the infantrymen crowded in the well of the boat, loaded with weaponry and ammunition, jammed together as tight as peas in a pod, shifting occasionally to relieve the cramping, as we churn endlessly forward, mile upon mile, hour after hour... to what ?

Two and a quarter years earlier, on 4 June 1940, when young Albert was still in school, British Prime Minister Winston Churchill had addressed a minute to his chiefs of staff. 'It is of the highest consequence to keep the largest numbers of German forces all along the coasts of the countries they have conquered, and we should immediately set to work to organize raiding forces on these coasts where the populations are friendly.... Surprise would be ensured by the fact that the destination would be concealed until the last moment.... An effort must be made to shake off the mental and moral prostration to the will and initiative of the enemy from which we suffer.'

Two days later, he expanded the concept. 'Enterprises must be prepared with specially-trained troops of the hunter class who can develop a reign of terror down these coasts, first of all on the "butcher and bolt" policy; but later on...we could surprise Calais or Boulogne, kill and capture the hun garrison, and hold the place until all the preparations to reduce it by siege or heavy storm have been made, and then away.'

*Able Seaman Albert Kirby, RCNVR.
'So relieved to be home. So happy
to be in one piece…. So angry that
I was even part of something so
confusing, agonizing, demanding,
and apparently unrewarding….'
[DND (Department of National
Defence)]*

Only three weeks after that, on the night of 23/24 June 1940 (a matter of days after the last elements of the 1st Canadian Infantry Division had been evacuated from Brest, and less than 48 hours after France's formal capitulation to the Germans) the first such raids took place. One hundred and twenty-five men of an Independent Company embarked in eight 'fast light motor boats' and approached the French shore at several points between Boulogne and Berck, twenty-five miles to the south.

Two parties landed on 'a waste of sand dunes where no living being was encountered'; another sneaked into a German seaplane anchorage but, finding the enemy alert, made no attempt to engage before sailing quietly home; and a fourth, after an hour on shore, was fired upon by a patrol of five Germans (who then fled) and withdrew with one officer superficially wounded.

The fifth party enjoyed slightly more success, indulging in a little butchery before they bolted. Landing just south of Le Touquet, they approached 'a large building' — probably a temporary barracks — surrounded by barbed wire. Two sentries were silently set upon and killed, 'but one of them cried out before he died', thus raising the alarm. Hurling grenades at the enemy, the raiders then 'withdrew without loss.'

Each party made its own way back to England, to various ports where their reception was mixed. At one place they were cheered ashore by sailors lining the rails of Royal Navy ships. At another, they were initially refused permission to enter harbour as no one there was sure of their identity. They lay off the harbour entrance, 'covered by guns on shore,' until they were all 'slightly intoxicated' on the contents of two jars of rum that just happened to be on board; and when they were finally allowed to land, they were arrested by military police who took them for deserters.

A minor setback. Combined Operations was soon a formal organization, commanded first by Lieutenant-General Sir Alan Bourne, then by a veteran of First World War raiding and favourite of Churchill's, Admiral of the Fleet Sir Roger Keyes. He was succeeded (from 27 October 1941) by the king's dashing young cousin, Commodore Lord Louis Mountbatten, who, at Churchill's behest, was shortly afterwards promoted to vice-admiral and (much to their annoyance) given a seat at the table of the prime minister's most senior military advisers, the chiefs of staff. Independent Companies became Special Service Battalions, and then Commandos.

Over the next two years there would be many more raids — some large, some small; some successful, some not. However, it is worth noting

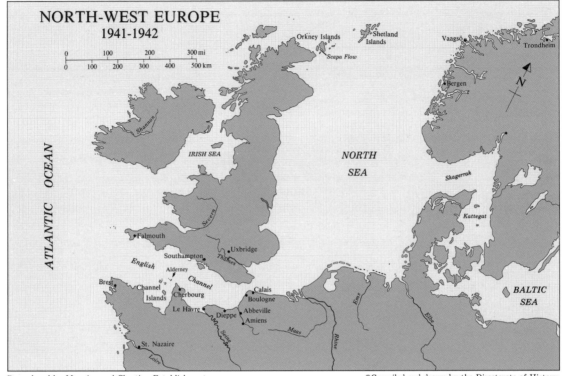

NORTH-WEST EUROPE
1941-1942

Orkney Islands
Shetland Islands
Scapa Flow
Vaagsö
Trondheim
Bergen

Shannon

IRISH SEA

NORTH SEA

Skagerrak

Kattegat

Severn

Falmouth

Uxbridge

Southampton

Thames

ATLANTIC OCEAN

English

Alderney

Channel

Brest

Channel Islands

Cherbourg

Calais

Boulogne

Le Havre

Dieppe

Abbeville

Amiens

Maas

BALTIC SEA

Ems

Rhine

Elbe

Seine

St. Nazaire

Loire

that, until the summer of 1942 (with one exception, as we shall see, in which the high cost was viewed as commensurate with the result), none of them were expensive in human terms. Failure usually meant a lack of success rather than defeat.

Gradually raiding became more sophisticated. A Christmas 1941 descent on Vaagsö, a fishing port on an island off the coast of southern Norway, was foreseen as an 'ambitious project against a defended area,' by Lieutenant-Colonel John Durnford-Slater, the commanding officer of N° 3 Commando, who would lead the assault. 'Undoubtedly,' he assured Mountbatten, 'there would be a violent enemy reaction.' There was a coastal defence battery of 'fairly heavy guns' to contend with on the island of Rugsundo, about four miles from Vaagsö. More dangerous might be the battery of four 125-mm pieces emplaced on the rocky islet of Maaloy just off the southern end of the town, covering the immmediate approaches. The German garrison was accurately estimated to be about 200 soldiers and 50 sailors, and they were to be attacked by some 525 commandos and a dozen officers and men of the Royal Norwegian Army.

There was also a danger from enemy aircraft. Intelligence sources predicted 20 to 30 bombers based about two hundred miles away, some at Stavanger and others at Trondheim, 'about 50 percent of these machines

being operationally serviceable at any given time.' Moreover, there was a squadron of Messerschmitt 109 fighters stationed at Herdla, only 80 miles down the coast, the first of which might reach Vaagso within an hour of an alarum.

Mountbatten was nervous. '"This seems to be very ambitious," he said. "Don't you think it would be better to take on something not quite so strong? How do you intend to deal with the [Maaloy] battery?" I said [reported Durnford-Slater]: "If you will allow the cruiser *Kenya* and her attendant destroyers to come right up to three thousand yards and give the battery a real pounding at first light, I am sure that problem will be disposed of. You can rely on our men to look after the German garrison."'

He could indeed. As dawn broke on 27 December — daylight hours were few at that latitude and at that time of year — *Kenya*'s twelve guns opened fire on Maaloy; in ten minutes, 'between four and five hundred six-inch shells fell upon a space not more than 250 yards square.' R-boats, loaded to the gunwales, had already been lowered from the two converted cross-Channel ferries that had carried the expedition from Scapa Flow, 'exactly one minute late' after a voyage of some 300 miles.

The need to neutralize the Maaloy position first had made it inevitable that the garrisons of the island and the

*Prime Minister Winston Churchill on the bridge of a Royal Navy warship.
'...we should immediately set to work to organize raiding forces on these
coasts where the populations are friendly.' [IWM (Imperial War Museum,
London)]*

*In Scotland, on a wet and windy July day, Prime Minister Winston
Churchill and (to his immediate right) his Combined Operations adviser,
Admiral of the Fleet Sir Roger Keyes, watch a practice landing in 1941.
[IWM]*

town got some warning of the raiders' approach. 'Only a hundred yards from shore, the agreed signal, a shower of Very lights, was sent up; the bombardment ceased immediately and then the [Handley Page] Hampdens... dropped their smoke bombs along the edge of the island, rapidly shrouding it in a pall of white smoke....' Throwing grenades and firing from the hip, commandos stormed ashore on Maaloy and at both ends of Vaagsö, a one-street town which straggled for three-quarters of a mile along the shore.

'Algy Forrester went off like a rocket... leaving a trail of dead Germans behind him,' recalled Durnford-Slater. Minutes later, Forrester (a newspaper correspondent in happier times) was dead, killed as he led an attack on the enemy headquarters in the Ulvesund Hotel.* The ranking Norwegian with the raiders, Captain Martin Linge, urged Forrester's troop on, only to meet the same fate. So, too, did Captain John Giles.

The commandos kept moving. 'It was very noisy,' Durnford-Slater noted, finding himself half-deafened by gunfire from *Kenya* and the soon-to-be silenced Rugsundo battery (*Kenya* was hit twice, without serious damage), the

howl of aircraft engines overhead, anti-aircraft fire from the four destroyers that had accompanied the expedition, the explosion of grenades and demolition charges, and the roar of the resulting flames. 'I heard one signaller complaining how difficult it was to receive messages. "This is bloody awful! A man can hardly hear himself think."'

He recorded that, 'at the peak period of the battle' his signallers were 'passing signals at the rate of forty an hour' to Brigadier Charles Haydon, the overall military commander, on board HMS *Kenya*. Nevertheless, many messages had to be repeated 'by visual means' because, when all the radio sets were in operation at once, 'there was all sorts of interference and static crackling in the receivers situated in such close proximity to one another on a bridge festooned with jury aerials.'

The Herdla airfield was attacked by 13 Bristol Blenheims and their bombs blew great holes in the wood-planked runway laid over Norwegian muskeg, 'into one of which an Me 109 fell just as it was about to take off, presumably for Vaagsö, with the rest of its squadron.' Over Vaagsö, relays of Bristol Beaufighters and fighter variants of the Blenheim — the only British fighters that had the range to do it — did their best to provide air cover 'from 9.28 in the morning until 4.15 in the evening by aircraft which had to fly some 350 miles to reach the scene of the fighting.'

---

* Eighteen months later, as Durnford-Slater was briefing his officers for the invasion of Sicily, he told them: 'You officers have got to set the pace once we get ashore.... Remember Vaagsö. Algy Forrester was the man who really won that one for us, by going like hell down the main street.'

Lord Louis Mountbatten, shortly after his appointment as Adviser, Combined Operations, inspecting commandos. He was, thought Robert Henriques, consumed by '...a vast ambition that was not reprehensible, because it exactly coincided with public interest....' [IWM]

British commandos returning from a pre-Dieppe raid. Note the customary woollen caps – the famed green beret was not introduced until the summer of 1942. [NAC (National Archives of Canada)]

Two of the Blenheims came from Nº 404 Squadron, RCAF, then based at Dyce, and during the morning they engaged a pair of Me 109s, driving them off and claiming one 'probably' and one 'possibly' destroyed. 'Smoke was observed coming from the engine of one which was losing height steadily as it drew away.' Their claims were unjustified, however. Four Heinkel 111s were shot down, but none of the Messerschmitts, in exchange for eight RAF machines.

British losses might have been less if everything had been done right. An over-confident Coastal Command, responsible for the air defence of the flotilla, had been too busy to practise its deck-to-air radio link between *Kenya* and the fighters. In the event, although communication with the Hampdens of Bomber Command (which had participated in rehearsals) was 'excellent,' the air controller on *Kenya* 'never once made contact with any of the five fighter sorties which arrived during the day.' At one moment, seamen watched in horror as the controller tried vainly to warn an unsuspecting Blenheim of the Me 109 that had slipped in below and behind it and that 'with one long contemptuous burst shot it out of the air.'

Half the German garrison was killed (including the commanding officer) and 98 men taken prisoner, for the loss of 21 raiders dead and 52 wounded. Key naval codes and cyphers were captured; 16,000 tons of shipping sunk; and a wireless station, an ammunition store, barracks and vehicle park, and a telephone exchange destroyed. Three fish-oil plants (their Vitamin D products vital to the wellbeing of U-boat crews) were burned to the ground, and 77 young Norwegians accepted a passage back to Scotland to join the Free Norwegian forces.

Even in small operations of such complexity, there must be an element of good luck if all is to go as well as it did at Vaagsö.* That raid's undoubted tactical success was, however, in the opinion of its 'patron,' Admiral Sir John Tovey, the commander of Britain's Home Fleet at Scapa Flow, 'achieved by sound planning and excellent inter-service co-operation, and by the assault force being well trained and equipped.' Fire support was appropriate, he might have added, navigation and timings were exact, communications adequate, and the landing force was not only well trained and rehearsed but also contained a strong nucleus of veteran, battle-hardened raiders.

No doubt Able Seaman Kirby would have known something of this, and of some other raids (for young sailors have been known to gossip), but he does not mention any of them in his memoir.

---

* 'In war something must be allowed to chance and fortune,' wrote General James Wolfe in 1757, 'seeing it is, in its nature, hazardous and an option of difficulties.'

Shortly after midnight, the moon had descended below the horizon and although the night was clear it was quite black. Suddenly, dead ahead of us, from the stern of R-84 came a flashing light, dot, dash, dash, dot, the Morse letter 'P'. S[ub]/L[ieutenan]t Leach saw it the same time as I did, and before I could say anything to him he warned me that that was the signal for refuelling.... I cut the throttle and we coasted to a stop. What a relief to cut that engine noise, a big cheer came up from all the Camerons as they began a major shift to relieve aching muscles and sore joints. Hop[per] and I jumped on to the upper deck and cut loose the gas cans and began pouring them into the two fuel tanks at the stern. A small flickering light appeared from down inside the craft, as though someone was trying to light a cigarette, and I shouted at the top of my voice, "For Christ's sake, put that bloody light out, we're pouring gasoline up here and the fumes will be running right down inside the well [of the boat]. Do you want to die even before you hit the beach ?' I said that still thinking we were headed for an exercise and quite unaware of our final destination.

After the Vaagsö raid had come the widely-publicized but somewhat atypical operation of 28 March 1942 on the French Atlantic coast at St. Nazaire. An ancient, obsolete destroyer, HMS *Campbeltown*, its bows packed with high explosives, had been driven into the lock gates of the largest drydock in Europe and subsequently blown up,

together with the pumping station for draining the dock. Both had been put out of commission for the rest of the war, so that the operation was accounted a success, even though none of the secondary aims had been achieved.

A complementary air attack by 60 heavy bombers had been included in the plan, intended to distract the defenders; but its execution was contingent upon clear visibility over the target, so that the minimum damage might be done to French civilians. Unfortunately, there was heavy cloud cover over St. Nazaire that night, and only four crews attempted to bomb the town. Moreover, their efforts came too early. 'Shortly afterwards the noise of planes died away altogether,' recalled a commando officer aboard the *Campbeltown*, just then entering the Loire estuary, 'and, one by one, the searchlights ahead of us were dimmed, leaving the coastline in darkness again.' Co-ordinating air bombardments with surface operations was a problem that would plague air and ground staffs to the end of the war.

The cost of St. Nazaire was horrendous. Nearly 80 percent of the 268 commandos and more than half of the 353 sailors who had set out from Falmouth failed to return. There, but for the grace of God, went Albert Kirby....

As a rule of thumb — and there were clear exceptions, such as the

A commando wireless operator charges ashore in the dawn's early light. Soldiers backpacking radios – easily distinguishable by their antennae – were the preferred targets of German snipers at Vaagsö and Dieppe. [IWM]

A burning fish oil plant, a fishing boat, and watchful commandos made for a dramatic picture at Vaagsö, 27 December 1941. [IWM]

Bruneval raid of 27/28 February 1942 to examine German radar capability — the degree of success in raids seems to have been directly related to the distance of each objective from that critical stretch of French coastline that lay between Boulogne and the Channel Islands. One mounted in April 1942, Operation ABERCROMBIE, included Canadian troops and illustrated perfectly this relationship between location and success or — as in this case — failure.

Fifty men of the Carleton and York Regiment, together with a rather larger number from Lord Lovat's Nº 4 Commando, set out to 'effect a landing on the French Coast under cover of darkness, reconnoitre Military Defences and beaches North and South of Hardelot [just south of Boulogne], attack and destroy Searchlight Post and return with prisoners and all available information.' The commandos were to land north of Hardelot, the Canadians south of it.

Nearly two years of experience and more than 50 similar jaunts had not made the raiders noticeably more competent than they had been in 1940, to judge by ABERCROMBIE. Lovat's men landed — though not at the right spot — and trotted off into the darkness to find and attack the searchlight battery. 'However, the recall rocket had to be fired before the searchlight post could be attacked and, as the enemy in the beach defences had incontinently fled, no prisoners were taken.'

The three boatloads of Canadians never even got ashore. Two of their RN crews lost contact with the third and none of them could find their assigned landing place. While they were all still seaching for it, the recall signal was seen and the three boats returned to Dover independently. 'It is doubtful whether the Germans had actually seen them,' wrote C.P. Stacey, 'and although machine-gun fire had been directed towards them they suffered no casualties.'

On board R-135, the Camerons' platoon commander began to remind his men of key points from an earlier briefing. *We expect the beach to be heavily defended, so we have to get across about ten or twenty yards of stony footing to reach a sea wall, our first cover, just as fast as possible. Taking cover behind this wall, we will organize our sections while Nº 1 Platoon finds the breach... that has been left by the South Saskatchewans. It is essential that we go through that breach the very second that we find it because, from that moment on, it will be a prime target for machine-gun fire....*

As I listen to him trying to make himself heard over the noise of the engine, a chill begins to creep over me as I slowly absorb the fact that we really are about to land on enemy territory. And even worse, the South Saskatchewan Regiment will be

Dieppe before the war,
photographed from the West
Headland, with vacationers
crowding what would become
(in 1942) Red and White Beaches.
The Casino is the large white
building in the upper centre of
the picture. [DND]

landing ahead of us so that the defences will already be in action by the time we hit the beach....

After a few minutes of trying to rationalize everything in my mind, I turned to the soldier beside me and asked 'Where in the hell are we going, anyway?' Somewhat startled, he fired back 'Don't you know? You're supposed to be taking us there. If you don't know, how in the hell are you going to get us there?'

'I don't need to know in order to get there, I'm just following the boat in front of me,' I replied. 'Don't worry about that, soldier, we'll get you there, on time and in the right place, but I'm just curious about where it is.'

It's a coastal town called Deepy,' he volunteered, 'somewhere in France.'

CHAPTER II

CHAPTER II

PLANNING AND PREPARATION: OPERATION RUTTER

The idea of a really major raid — something similar to, but significantly greater than, that on Vaagsö — had long been in the air. As early as 23 June 1941 (the day after the German invasion of the Soviet Union) Churchill had suggested such a raid on the Pas de Calais. He had vaguely proposed 'something on the scale of twenty-five thousand to thirty thousand men — perhaps the Commandos plus one of the Canadian divisions.'

That concept had been promptly dismissed by his chiefs of staff, but only four months later, on 18 October, they had authorized the commander-in-chief, Home Forces, to carry out a whole range of offensive operations from 'small informative raids' to 'major operations on the Continent.' In between those extremes came 'large informative and destructive raids, up to two nights and a day', and even raids by 'one or two divisions.'

Of course, that authorization was really no more than a generalized permission, falling a long way short of the specific chiefs of staff approval required for a major raid. At the same time, it was deemed important to start increasing the scale and complexity of raids. Vaagsö had been the first of Mountbatten's attempts — followed by the uncharacteristic attack on

St Nazaire — and the idea of a larger raid on Alderney, second smallest of the permanently inhabited Channel Islands and the closest one to Britain,* was proposed early in March 1942.

The first few Landing Craft Tanks, or LCTs, able to carry three of the new Churchill tanks, were now available, so that armour could be included in the raiding force. In April some two thousand commandos and British infantry, together with two squadrons of Churchills, assembled on the Isle of Wight and began training for an attack on Alderney, under the codename BLAZING; but 'differences of opinion' arose between the air and ground commanders and, on 6 May, that operation was cancelled.

However, there were now other reasons for raiding on a larger scale, besides those adumbrated by Churchill in 1940. To the chagrin of the prime minister (not to mention Parliament and people), in early February 1942 the German battlecruisers at Brest, *Scharnhorst* and *Gneisenau*, together with the heavy cruiser *Prinz Eugen*,

---

* The Channel Islands – primarily Jersey, Guernsey, Alderney and Sark – have been British territory uninterruptedly since the thirteenth century. They were the only parts of the United Kingdom to be occupied by the enemy during the Second World War.

had slipped through the English Channel into the Baltic Sea, from whence (together with the battleship *Tirpitz*, already moored in a Norwegian fjord) they threatened the critical convoy routes to Russia. On the Eastern Front, a Russian winter counter-offensive had laboured to a halt without making much impact, and the *Wehrmacht* was setting itself up for another *Blitzkrieg* once the ground had dried out. (Worse things had happened in the Far East — in the Philippines, Malaya, the Netherlands East Indies and Burma — but those events had no impact on raiding policy.)

Whether the Russians could, or would, hold on without a Second Front in the west was a question that loomed large in Anglo-American minds, for a distrustful Stalin was giving out mixed signals. On 23 February he had publicly declared that 'the Red Army [had] no intention of exterminating the German nation and of destroying the German state.' It was not hard to read into his words the possibility of a compromise peace if his Allies failed to bear what was, in his eyes, a fair share of the burden.

Consequently, a conceivable need to support the Russians by establishing a Second Front in France, either in the Pas de Calais or on the Cherbourg peninsula, was worrying the Anglo-American political and military leadership. No one was very happy with the idea, although the chiefs of staff accepted that, if the Russian situation worsened enough, '[they] might be compelled to do this and must in any case prepare for it.'

The brunt of establishing such a bridgehead (codenamed SLEDGEHAMMER for the moment) would have to be borne by the British if it was to be implemented in 1942, for the Americans — at war for less than five months — were still fully occupied in expanding their instructional cadres and training initial intakes. However, both Churchill and Sir Alan Brooke, the chief of the imperial general staff, had growing doubts about the large-scale fighting ability of the British Army. Excuses were plentiful, and freely offered, but in Norway, France, Greece and Crete their troops had been soundly thrashed, often by numerically inferior forces. Even in the Western Desert, where the British, by and large, enjoyed substantial intelligence, *matériel* and logistical advantages, their record was inconsistent, to say the least. Could British soldiers take and hold a substantial bridgehead in the face of resolute counter-attacks?

A more concrete limitation on SLEDGEHAMMER revolved about logistics. The planning staffs had grave doubts about the possibility of taking a port — even a smallish port — without the harbour being blocked and its facilities being destroyed, either in the course of the fighting or through enemy demolitions. Nor were there enough specialized landing craft

Vice-Admiral Lord Louis Mountbatten, described as a War Lord 'with no weakness except a total inability to judge men correctly, whether they were his cronies or his subordinates,' questions a soldier while inspecting Canadians at a Combined Operations training centre in 1942. [IWM]

The Chief of the Imperial General Staff, Field Marshal Sir Alan Brooke, makes a point to a stone-faced First Lord of the Admiralty, A.V. Alexander. [IWM]

available in the spring of 1942, or in prospect during the summer, to supply a large force over open beaches for any length of time.

Such a venture would call for what the Royal Navy labelled Landing Craft Mechanized (LCMs), capable of carrying up to seventeen tons of supplies, and Landing Craft Assault (LCAs) — armour-plated successors to the R-boat — as well as LCTs. All three types (and several variants of each) were now being built, both in Britain and the United States, but in the realm of naval construction priority had to go to convoy escort vessels if North American production of foodstuffs, oil and weapons of war were to continue, as they must, reaching Britain and Russia.

Of course, if a port could be taken with its major facilities intact, the shortage of landing craft would not be vital. But could it? A short-term raid might provide the answer, and it was most probably that prospect that led Mountbatten's staff to consider the possibility of a raid on Dieppe.

The selection of Dieppe seems to have been based upon the size of the port, the perceived strength of its defences, and, most importantly, on its distance from England. It was not as strongly held as Boulogne or Calais, and it lay just 70 miles from the English coast, within the limits of effective fighter cover.

An account of the planning process, prepared some months after the raid, claims that there were originally two alternative outline plans. One contemplated a frontal assault, combined with subsidiary attacks on both sides of the town, at Puys and Pourville. The other proposed relying entirely on flank attacks, with infantry landings at Puys and Pourville and the tanks being put ashore at Quiberville, six miles to the west.

In both scenarios, paratroops would be dropped to neutralize the coastal defence batteries at Berneval (three 170 mm and four 105 mm guns) and Varengeville (six 150 mm guns), which would otherwise be able to shell the landing areas. And both were built around the concept of a 'two-tide' raid lasting as long as 15 hours.

Subsequently, the first concept was adopted in the Outline Plan, since 'on balance there were advantages in taking the town by a frontal assault.' Flank landings, it was held, 'would make a surprise attack on the town more difficult to achieve'; and if the tanks were landed at Quiberville they 'would have to cross three rivers' to reach Dieppe. Actually, there were only two rivers to cross, the Saane and the Scie, and French historian Jacques Mordal has rightly described them as brooks rather than rivers, 'no more than 30 feet wide and three feet deep.' Ask any of the inhabitants of the region which would appear to them the more difficult — to land tanks on a

Men of the Essex Scottish learn house-clearing techniques on an English
barn as part of their preparations for Dieppe. Few of them would find
the opportunity to practice their new-found skills on 19 August 1942.
[NAC]

On a gray winter day, Canadian
soldiers practice 'fire and
movement' exercises beneath a
wooded hillside. Strangely, they
are wearing battle order (small
pack, etc.) but not wearing
helmets. [NAC]

defended beach like that of Dieppe or to cross the Rivers Saane and Scie — and their reply would be unanimous.

Later, after the Dieppe raid, the Germans flooded the valley [sic] by closing the sluice gates at the points where these small watercourses flowed beneath the dyke on the sea front. In 1942 they had not yet thought of taking this precaution.... Nor were the bridges mined and, in the event of a surprise landing, they would have been as easy to take [by accompanying infantry] as all the other points of the road which runs close to the beach.

For a while the idea was retained of landing one squadron of tanks east of the Scie, at Pourville, where there was a short beach between the mouth of the river and the cliff of Dieppe's west headland, but by 21 April that alternative, too, had been abandoned. A primarily frontal assault on the town by two infantry battalions and a regiment of tanks would be preceded by a heavy air bombardment, someone had decided. (This 'someone' was probably Lieutenant-General Sir Bernard Montgomery, who, as we shall see shortly, apparently had come into the RUTTER chain of command the previous day.)

Much would depend upon achieving a degree of surprise, and on the short hooks from Puys and Pourville by two battalions assigned to 'taking out' the dominating headlands on each side of the town. The West Headland included a German radar station that was one of the main objectives of the raid. Additionally, a fifth battalion would land at Pourville, to drive inland and, linking up with the tanks that would have come through the town, take the enemy's divisional headquarters — wrongly believed to be at Arques-la-Bataille, four miles inland — and the airfield at St. Aubin, on the high ground just to the west of Arques. The airfield (which might better have been called an airstrip) was simply a waypoint for liaison aircraft and the like, and had little apparent relevance to any conceivable air operations. Why it should have been included among the *sixteen* specified objectives of the raid has never been explained.

Notably absent, even at this early stage of planning, was any weight of naval fire support. Mountbatten had asked the Admiralty for a battleship to support the raid. With nearly 600 Spitfires dedicated to the provision of air cover and, at best, only 120 enemy fighters available to provide protection for his bombers or torpedo-bombers, there was surely little danger from the air.

Even if the risk had been deemed too great to imperil such major units as *King George V* or *Duke of York,* lying at Gibraltar was HMS *Malaya,* of 1915 vintage and thus too slow (at 20 knots) for fleet operations, but still with eight 15-inch guns. Nevertheless, the response of the First Sea Lord, Sir Dudley Pound (perhaps recalling the fate of *Prince of Wales* and *Repulse,*

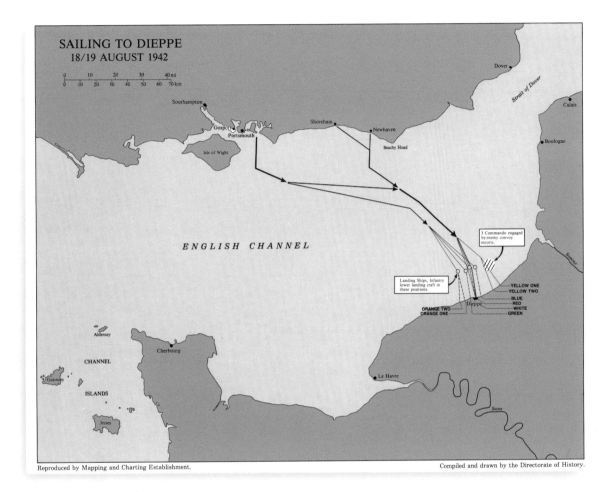

SAILING TO DIEPPE
18/19 AUGUST 1942

while forgetting that they had been caught without any air cover at all) was unequivocal. 'A battleship in the Channel! Dicky, you must be mad!'*

The navy also had two 15-inch gun monitors in commission — slow, specialized bombardment vessels which could certainly have done the job — but they were both in the Far East. There were, in plenty, heavy cruisers with 8-inch main armaments, lighter cruisers (such as *Kenya*, which had been so effective at Vaagsö) with their 6-inch guns, and fleet destroyers with 4.7s. However, the Admiralty was apparently unwilling to hazard anything more than eight Hunt Class destroyer-escorts, each armed with four high-angle 4-inch guns which could be used for anti-aircraft defence as well as for bombardment.

So much for naval participation — or lack of it. The air force, pushed by Sir Charles Portal, the RAF's chief of air staff, was initially more co-operative. For more than a year now, his Fighter Command, under Air Marshal Sir Sholto Douglas, had been 'leaning forward into France,' trying to bring the *Luftwaffe* to battle on favourable terms; and during all that time the *Jagdflieger* had been picking up the gauntlet only when circumstances suited them. The overall result had been a loss ratio of approximately 4:1 in favour of the Germans and virtually no attrition of their fighter force, but in Operation RUTTER there was the prospect of *compelling* the enemy to fight and inflicting major losses on him.

Substituting for the missing battleship, Bomber Command's Sir Arthur Harris reluctantly agreed to a pre-dawn air raid involving some 120 heavy bombers that would — theoretically — wreak havoc on German defences and communications, perhaps confusing the enemy without revealing that an amphibious assault was to follow. Five light bomber squadrons (Bostons and Blenheims) and two fighter-bomber squadrons (Hurri-bombers) would attack artillery batteries immediately before the landing and during the day, as well as lay smoke during the troops' final approach to shore; while 56 squadrons of fighters (48 of Spitfires, six of Hurricanes, two of the new Hawker Typhoons) would provide diversions, protection from the *Luftwaffe*, and close support for the ground forces.

---

* In September and October 1940 the battleship *Revenge* had been used to bombard the port of Cherbourg, and the monitor *Erebus* used against coastal batteries in the Pas de Calais. Twenty years after the fact, Rear-Admiral H.T. Baillie-Grohman, the Naval Force commander for RUTTER, explained to the Royal Navy's official historian that when he had asked Mountbatten 'why we could not have a battleship,' he had been told that 'there were propaganda reasons, and W[inston] S[pencer] C[hurchill] at the bottom of it.' Even in 1962, Baillie-Grohman felt that 'it would make the Canadians furious if they knew this. And I would not blame them. So you would agree, I think...that even on the principle of historical truth, it would not be politic to let it out, even now.'

On the left, the evil genius of Dieppe, Captain John Hughes-Hallett, DSO, commanding HMS Eagle in December 1944. [IWM]

Although Combined Operations Headquarters (COHQ) was responsible for planning raids and experimenting in amphibious warfare, as we have noted, a 1941 chiefs of staff directive had given the ultimate authority for carrying them out to the commander-in-chief, Home Forces, who in 1942 was General Sir Bernard Paget. On 21 March, however, Mountbatten — who had been promoted to the rank of vice-admiral and advanced from Adviser, Combined Operations to Chief of Combined Operations (CCO) three days earlier, with a seat on the Chiefs of Staff Committee — had persuaded Paget to delegate that authority to him, on the condition that 'a fair proportion of Home Forces' would be incorporated in major raids.

That meant, of course, that Home Forces would still have to be included in the planning process, and their views given due weight to the extent that their troops would be involved. But why should Paget have given up his Command's sole high-profile offensive role to the upstart Mountbatten? Nigel Hamilton, Montgomery's biographer, has suggested that 'the only explanation can be found in Mountbatten's personality and his high connections, both with the Royal Family and with Churchill.'

In any case, mounting the proposed raid was now essentially Mountbatten's business but non-commando troops must be employed, if only to meet his

agreement with Paget. Once again Paget delegated, this time appropriately keeping control within the Home Forces 'shop.' He assigned Home Forces' interest to the commander of his South-Eastern Command, an officer widely respected for his professional approach to soldiering and generally disliked for his brusque, acerbic manner.

That 'efficient little shit' Sir Bernard Montgomery (as a fellow officer described him) had taken up his current appointment on 17 November 1941, and from that date the Canadian Corps had been one of the formations under his command. Thus he was well aware of the Canadians' strengths and weaknesses. Indeed, he had gone through the senior officer cadres of the Canadian divisions with a fine comb, demanding that Lieutenant-General H.D.G. Crerar, the corps commander,[*] weed out the old and unfit.

Although nothing was ever charged against his competence, among those who had gone was 62-year-old Major-General Victor Odlum of the 2nd Division, replaced by John Hamilton Roberts, eleven years younger. Roberts, like Crerar and General A.G.L. McNaughton (who took command of First Canadian Army, on returning from sick leave, when it was formed on 5 April 1942) was a gunner by trade.

---

[*] Lieutenant-General A.G.L. McNaughton was nominally the corps commander until 5 April, but he had been on sick leave since 14 November 1941.

The unreality of much training is illustrated in this picture of men of Les Fusiliers Mont-Royal taking aim at a fictitious enemy on a clifftop. Their rifles are bolt-action Lee-Enfields, little changed from those their fathers carried up Vimy Ridge. [NAC]

Looking every inch the warrior king he was not, soldier-scientist General A.G.L. McNaughton considers a point made by a subordinate commander in the course of a training exercise. [NAC]

As a junior officer in the First World War he had served on the Western Front for three years, been wounded, and been awarded a Military Cross. Then, after an entirely undistinguished inter-war career, he had risen from commanding an artillery regiment to commanding an infantry division in only sixteen months, without ever having held a command in battle.

In the brigades and battalions, too, older officers and non-commissioned officers, inevitably less physically fit than younger men but sometimes with battle experience in the First World War, had been ruthlessly rejected in favour of sharp young soldiers who had never been under fire. In Roberts' 2nd Division, for example, the commanders of the two brigades that would go to Dieppe were Sherwood Lett, aged 46 (who also had an MC from the First War) and William Southam, aged 41. The average age of the battalion commanders at Dieppe would be thirty-six.

Montgomery was apparently (there is nothing in writing) handed Paget's residual responsibility for RUTTER when he visited GHQ Home Forces on 20 April. The decision for a frontal assault came on the 21st, and at some uncertain point between that date and the 30th he met with Crerar and suggested to him that the Canadians might play the major role. That, of course, was short-circuiting the proper chain of command. His first approach should have been to McNaughton, as army commander and senior Canadian officer overseas. But Montgomery knew that Crerar was desperately keen to see his men in action under almost any circumstances, while McNaughton, preoccupied with national concerns, favoured a more cautious approach which reflected Prime Minister Mackenzie King's anxiety to avoid squandering Canadian lives and so keep the conscription issue off the political agenda.

Montgomery had been watching the Canadians on exercises earlier that month, and had concluded that Roberts was 'the best divisional commander in the corps' and his GSO 1, or chief of staff, Lieutenant-Colonel Churchill Mann, was 'first class.' He had already decided, as a result of earlier inspections, that the 2nd was now the best of the Canadian divisions, and that the 4th and 6th Brigades were distinctly better than the 5th. No doubt he instructed Crerar — putty in his hands, as far as military matters were concerned — which formations to nominate for the proposed raid.

The basis for the selection of the 14th Army Tank Regiment (The Calgary Regiment) over the 11th (The Ontario Regiment) and 12th (Three Rivers Regiment) is less clear. It may have been, in the best Canadian political tradition, merely geographical — Ontario and Quebec were already represented in the infantry components; Alberta was not. Or it may simply have been assessed by

Montgomery or Crerar as the best trained of the three Army Tank Brigade units. Lieutenant-Colonel J.C. Andrews was a 33-year-old regular soldier, a Royal Military College graduate generally considered to be an outstanding officer who had brought his regiment to a higher pitch of training than the others.

McNaughton only heard what was happening on 30 April when Montgomery told him that he had been 'pressed to agree' to a composite British and Canadian force (presumably by Mountbatten) but felt it essential to maintain unity of command. The Canadians were, in his opinion, 'those best suited' to the job. They were certainly as well suited as any division in Home Forces. Those British formations still in the United Kingdom that had fought in 1940, no longer had a sufficient cadre of veterans serving in them to qualify as 'battle-hardened.' Too many of those who had, metaphorically, 'seen the elephant' in Norway or Holland and France, had since been posted out and were now seeing real elephants in Burmese jungles, or jerboas — desert rats — in North Africa.

Bearing in mind that the Canadians had lots of training but virtually no one (who was likely to go into combat) with actual battle experience, it might be thought that McNaughton and Crerar were, nevertheless, too free in their willingness to volunteer men for such a hazardous enterprise. In the United States, the army's chief of staff, General George Marshall, was worrying about what would happen when his men had to go into battle. Briefing Colonel Lucian Truscott, prior to posting him and a small group of American officers to Mountbatten's Richmond Terrace headquarters in May 1942, he explained that:

> ...there could be no substitute for actual battle in preparing men pyschologically to meet the nervous tensions and uncertainties of combat....
>
> It was primarily for this reason, he continued, that he had arranged with Admiral Mountbatten to send [Truscott's] group to London. Raids...would be increased in scope and in frequency until the time for the invasion. As many American soldiers as possible would be given an opportunity to participate in these operations. [Truscott's] task would be to arrange for this participation and for dissemination of this battle experience among assault units.

No such thoughts appear to have entered the minds of McNaughton or Crerar. McNaughton gave his approval to arrangements already made, and Churchill Mann quickly put together the first Canadian evaluation of the plan. Mustering the pros and cons, as he saw them, he concluded that 'it seems to have a reasonable prospect of success' and announced himself as 'in favour of adopting the outline plan.'

Mann was looked upon as one of the brightest minds in the Canadian Army. Married to a daughter of Colonel R.S. McLaughlin of McLaughlin-Buick fame, he had been among those forward-looking officers who had experimented with motorized soldiering in pre-war days. If any Canadian could recognize the unlikelihood of moving tanks through the narrow streets of a medieval town just after it had been bombed, as opposed to moving them over open country and across two shallow streams, it should have been him — and, indeed, the danger of debris blocking their way was noted in his appreciation. However, he also saw the frontal attack as an advantage. *'It, if successful, puts the A[rmoured] F[ighting] V[ehicles] in easy striking distance of the most appropriate objectives for their employment.'*

First Roberts, then Crerar, and finally McNaughton, approved of his conclusion. It needs to be remembered, however, that despite the experience of raiding that COHQ had accumulated over the past two years, there was still no formal doctrine for amphibious operations in the way that there was for such other aspects of tactics as an advance to contact, a set-piece attack, or a withdrawal while in contact with the enemy. The only expertise lay in COHQ, where Mountbatten's enormous enthusiasm and somewhat slapdash approach held sway; and no Canadian had either the

theoretical training or the practical experience that might have encouraged him to propose revisions to, much less reject, its plans.

At the same time, these were all ambitious men seeking to enhance their reputations and further their careers. To have declined to participate on any grounds other than that of an absurdly and demonstrably unreasonable plan would have been tantamount to professional suicide for Mann, Roberts and Crerar, and would have done McNaughton little good in the public eye, had word of it got out. Back in Canada, after three years of war and very little army involvement,[*] many a bloodthirsty politician and journalist was waiting to pounce. And so, on 15 May, McNaughton cabled Ottawa:

> Outline Plan has been approved by Chiefs of Staff Committee. I am satisfied (a) objective is worthwhile (b) land forces detailed are sufficient (c) sea and air forces adequate (d) arrangements for co-operation satisfactory. I have therefore accepted this outline plan and authorized detailed planning to proceed.

The actual raid commanders had already been appointed on 9 May — Roberts for ground operations, Air Vice-Marshal Sir Trafford Leigh-Mallory of Fighter Command's Nº 11 Group for air, and Rear-Admiral H.T.

---

[*] The notable exception being that of Hong Kong, in which General Crerar was also a major player.

*Lieutenant-General Bernard Law
Montgomery, general officer commanding, South-Eastern Command,
inspects the South Saskatchewan
Regiment, 22 February 1942. 'I
am satisfied that the operation
[JUBILEE] as planned is a possible
one and has good prospects of
success...,' he would write five
months later, condemning many
of them to death, mutilation, or
two-and-a-half years of prison life.
The frontal assault on Dieppe was
Montgomery's choice. [NAC]*

47

Baillie-Grohman (the Navy's expert in amphibious operations, who was to be brought back from the Middle East for the occasion) for sea.

Detailed planning took the form of deciding who should do what to whom. As far as the Canadians were concerned, intelligence appreciations indicated 'that Dieppe [was] not heavily defended....' It was garrisoned by 'one infantry battalion.... supported by some 500 Divisional and Regimental troops. Personnel of Anti-Aircraft and Coastal Defence Batteries total[led] 1,500 (approximately).' The reports went on:

> Three 4-gun troops are sited right left and centre, behind the town. Possibly they are three troops making up a battery of field gun/howitzers....
>
> There is no infantry on either side of the town. There is one troop of coastal artillery to the East, and one to the West, each being some three miles away from the town defences.
>
> ...It is probable that one reinforced rifle company holds the town east of the River Arques [including the East Headland and Puys], another the town west of the River Arques [including the West Headland] and another the area [at Pourville] around the mouth of the river Scie.
>
> This distributes the observed pillboxes in the proportion of 12:18:11, total 31 [sic]; there are in all 48 machine guns in the battalion.

The mathematics of enemy pillboxes — an absolutely vital matter to the assaulting infantry — illustrate very well the slapdash nature of much

of the work carried out at Mountbatten's headquarters. His intelligence staff was headed by Wing Commander the Marquis of Casa Maury, a wealthy pre-war playboy and amateur racing driver, none of whose qualifications, except for a certain facility with languages, were appropriate to his appointment. By all accounts, Richmond Terrace, where COHQ was located, was full of such people. That hardy fighting man, Shimi Lovat, visiting there to be briefed on JUBILEE, would recall that it 'swarmed with red-tabbed gentlemen.'

> The bee-hive illusion was enhanced by busy passages, honeycombed with rooms filled with every branch of the services, including the powder-puff variety, who looked elegant in silk stockings. There was said to be a fair proportion of drones among the inmates. Signing a pass allowed the visitor, having stated his business, to sit around talking to pretty Wrens, or out on the terrace when it wasn't raining.... As a port of call, Combined Ops was not favoured by the serving officer.

Finally, it was estimated that 'within 3-8 hours' the Dieppe garrison could be reinforced by 'one battalion from the south; one battalion from the west; two companies from along the coast; Divisional troops from direction Arques = 2,500.' After eight hours there could be 'two battalions and regimental troops from Rouen; one battalion from direction Arques = 2,400' on the scene, and after 15 hours — by which

Churchill tanks of the Calgary Regiment on the Isle of Wight, June 1942. The Calgaries took two versions of the Churchill to Dieppe – one with a 2-pdr gun in a cast turret, and one with a 6-pdr in a welded turret. Both boasted armour that proved impenetrable to German weapons. [DND]

time the raiders should have re-embarked — 'armoured forces from direction Paris' might be arriving.

British paratroopers would deal with the coast artillery batteries on both flanks, at Berneval and Varengeville. The Royal Regiment of Canada, together with one company of the Black Watch (Royal Highland Regiment) of Canada, would land on Blue Beach (Puys) in order to secure the Eastern Headland; while the South Saskatchewan Regiment would land on Green Beach (Pourville) to take the Western Headland and the low, wooded ridge that ran inland on the other side of the Scie valley. Both those assaults were timed for 'the beginning of nautical twilight,' or, in landlubber's terms, that pre-dawn moment when, on a clear moonless night, the stars could still be seen and the horizon was just becoming discernable.

Following the South Saskatchewans ashore (to the dismay of Able Seaman Kirby) would be the Queen's Own Cameron Highlanders, who were to advance up the valley to take the airstrip at St. Aubin and the divisional headquarters believed to be at Arques.

In front of Dieppe, *an hour after the flank attacks* — by which time the two headlands should have been taken by the flanking forces — the Essex Scottish would land on the left (Red Beach) and the Royal Hamilton Light Infantry on the right (White Beach),

both backed up by the 14th Canadian Army Tank Regiment (Calgary Regiment). In reserve would be Les Fusiliers Mont-Royal, and the Royal Marine Commando which had been assigned to collect up the invasion barges in the harbour and, if possible, sail them back to England. If not, they were to destroy them.

Spread among them all, but concentrated on Red and White Beaches, would be seven officers and 307 other ranks of the Royal Canadian Engineers, mostly assigned to demolition tasks, and 14 officers and 256 other ranks of the Royal Canadian Artillery (some of whom had been trained to operate captured enemy guns).

A number of smaller groups would also be involved. There would be ten officers and 116 men of the Royal Canadian Army Medical Corps, five officers and 120 men of the Toronto Scottish (specialists equipped with belt-fed medium machine-guns), a forty-strong element of the Canadian Provost Corps and detachments of the Service, Ordnance and Intelligence Corps, together with 'miscellaneous small units and detachments' and a few brave men of the Inter-Allied Commando — mostly native German speakers assigned to specialist intelligence-gathering.

Distributed throughout the force (including the two Commandos assigned to take the flanking heavy coastal batteries) would be 50 US Army Rangers — American commandos — the first fruits of Lucian Truscott's mission. And last, but not least, there was an RAF technician, Flight Sergeant Jack Nissenthal, whose sole business lay with the radar devices on the West Headland and whose South Saskatchewan escorts were instructed to make sure that he did not, under any circumstances, fall into enemy hands!

By 20 May the whole of the Canadian force was on the Isle of Wight and security ensured by monitoring all communication with the mainland (even though none of the troops involved knew yet where they would be going or when). Although the men were already fit, since nothing is more physically exhausting than fear and every normal man will be afraid in battle, much emphasis was placed on physical fitness. The 4th Brigade's commander, Sherwood Lett, First World War soldier, Rhodes scholar and peace-time lawyer, summed it up in a moving letter to his wife — made all the more poignant by what would happen to them eight weeks later.

The men are very keen and enthusiastic. The new training hours are 7-12 am and 1-5 pm and three or four nights a week. I have been out all day every day and each evening but one, covering each battalion right down to companies twice each day.... It makes for a long day, for we are usually busy again in the evenings either watching night training or planning further programmes....

I never cease to marvel at the things these men of ours can do. Nothing seems impossible to them now. This week I have watched them for hours do things which even six or eight months ago they would have thought impossible themselves. They are hard and fit and skilful in their work.... They have been soaked to the skin and caked with mud and yet you see them, whistling their way along the narrow roads, marching miles on end in pouring rain.

I still get a lump in my throat when I see men marching. You would think I would get over that after all these years, but I never have. When I watch a thousand men march past I always see their faces and their eyes, and their clothing and shoes and their armament and bearing, and all the things an inspecting officer should see. But I also, always, see a thousand wives and mothers and fathers and sweethearts and kiddies shouting and waving....

A thousand marching men represent so much — so many people and so many things. And it always takes me back to the last war when we used to march past Currie or Byng or Rawlinson.... Our men always marched with such confidence and assurance. And they do the same today. They are a splendid lot.

Training carried on — without naming names or places — for specific, raid-oriented functions, some of which were relevant and some of which were not. The experience of the Royals was probably typical.

For the next few weeks they occupied themselves with obstacle courses, bayonet fighting, unarmed combat, cliff climbing, firing from the hip, embarking and disembarking from landing craft, demolition practice, and river crossings by breeches buoy....

The next week the tempo of training increased. Attacks were staged in co-operation with tanks; all ranks learned to swim fully clothed; instruction was given in the grenade and the sub-machine gun and in the improvised transportation of the wounded; rapid marching and night marching by compass bearing were practiced. On 1 June the Regiment marched to Yarmouth, boarded landing craft, was carried to Colwell Bay [still on the Isle of Wight], landed in two waves, and then retired again under cover of a smokescreen.

The South Saskatchewans recalled especially practising 'the breaching of wire obstacles' with Bangalore torpedoes — lengths of explosive-filled pipe which could be pushed forward into coils of barbed wire and then exploded to blow holes through which men could pass. None of the regimental histories, however, nor any of the memoirs this author has seen, record that anyone was impressing on them what the commandos already knew to be the most important single tactic for raiders to remember — to get off the beach as quickly as possible, no matter what the immediate cost. 'Algy Forrester was off like a rocket...,' Durnford-Slater had noted at Vaagsö....

While the fighting soldiers trained, commanders and staff officers planned, but Montgomery seems to have taken curiously little interest in what was going on. He was, of course, subordinate in rank and appointment to Mountbatten, a man for whom he had no professional (and probably no personal) respect. Having chosen the troops and stipulated a frontal assault, his extraordinary vanity may well have driven him to divorce himself as much as possible from everything else to do with the raid.

Indeed, it may be that he — and he alone — in some obscure way, covertly hoped that the raid might fail. If he could then lay the blame on Mountbatten, he would have brought low a man who, in his harshly professional view, probably deserved such an end. The only meeting of the Planning Committee that he personally attended (as opposed to sending a representative) was held on 5 June, when he presided and Mountbatten was not present. The latter was in the United States, explaining to Roosevelt and General Marshall why the British felt a Second Front was impracticable, and his acolyte, Hughes-Hallett, was there with him.

Baillie-Grohman had now arrived from the Middle East, however, and all three force commanders were on hand when the proposed heavy air bombardment was eliminated from the Detailed Plan at the suggestion of Leigh-Mallory — though, as we shall

Churchill tanks lined up before a training exercise, July 1942. Operation JUBILEE marked the first occasion when armoured fighting vehicles were used in an amphibious operation. [NAC]

see, it is unlikely that the idea was his. Baillie-Grohman, the acknowledged expert, apparently said nothing. In fact, writing to the Royal Navy's official historian, Captain S.W. Roskill, 20 years later, he could not remember attending the meeting. 'If it was held, I must have been there, but I don't remember a thing about it now.... I must have left the meeting with a good many reservations.'

He went on to explain that the chief factor 'which caused me not to make much more fuss than I did [over the abolition of heavy bombing] was a signal (or message) arriving at Cowes soon after 1st June, which was to this effect — "The heavy air bombardment of Dieppe in support of the landing there is cancelled, as it is against the policy of H[is] M[ajesty's] Government to damage French towns (at night?)."' Some discussion about abandoning the bombing had, in fact, occurred during the previous meeting, at which Mountbatten had been present. Churchill, anxious to retain French goodwill, had only reluctantly given permission for the bombing, and it is perfectly possible that, on second thoughts, he had now withdrawn it. However, no copy of the signal seems to have survived the years.

In October 1942, Roberts would note (in a letter to Major-General P.J. Montague at Overseas Headquarters), that his acquiescence had been based on a (new-found) belief that such bombing might make the streets of the town impassable to armour. Now that the air bombardment was to be deleted, what was to replace it? 'It was agreed that cannon fighters should attack the beach defences and the high ground on either side of Dieppe as the first flight of landing craft were coming in to land.'

Montgomery still seems to have been quite unconcerned by what was now a conspicuous lack of fire support. Never one to let the truth damage his image, however, in his *Memoirs* Montgomery flatly denied any responsibility, suggesting that the bombing program, like the paratroop assaults, was not eliminated until the raid was re-mounted as JUBILEE — when he was out of the picture. 'I should not myself have agreed with these changes,' he wrote. 'The demoralization of the enemy forces by preliminary bombing was essential (as was done in Normandy in 1944 just before the troops touched down on the beaches).'

Faced with such blatant lying, the artless historian can only reiterate (while pointing out that on D-Day preliminary heavy bombing of the beaches was relatively ineffective) that Montgomery was present when the bombing program was dropped and, according to the minutes, made no objection. If he had spoken up his dissent would most certainly have been recorded.

One of the five tanks equipped with a chespaling track-laying device immediately prior to Operation JUBILEE. [DND]

Training was building to a climax. On 12 June the troops all embarked for Exercise YUKON, a full-scale rehearsal carried out at West Bay, near Bridport in Dorsetshire, on a stretch of coast resembling that at Dieppe, with Generals Paget, McNaughton and Crerar in attendence. It was a shambles. Infantry units were landed miles from their assigned beaches and the Calgarys arrived at their destination over an hour late.

The tanks were eventually landed on a shale beach not at all like the loose shingle they would meet at Dieppe; but on the Dieppe-like shingle of Chesil Bank, some miles to the east, divisional engineers under Major B. Sucharov were busy testing the ability of a Churchill to cope with that kind of surface. Handled carefully, their tank did not sink into the shingle, and it seemed there was no great risk of pebbles catching between sprocket and track and jamming or breaking the latter. On this kind of loose surface, it was able to climb a gradient of 1 in 4 without difficulty but could not handle 1 in 2.5.

The gradient at Dieppe varied from time to time, and from place to place, as the shingle was shifted by storm waves, but it would not normally exceed 1 in 4. However, when working from a loose shingle base sloping up to a sea wall, the tank could not manage its normal vertical 'step' performance of two and a half feet. It seemed that the best

way for the tanks to reach the esplanade would be for sappers to blow gaps in the wall with high-explosive charges, but efforts to find a better solution continued.

*

* *

Meanwhile, Josef Stalin was still unhappy and complaining about the Anglo-American inability (or unwillingness, as he saw it) to open a Second Front. In mid-May there was pressure all along the Eastern Front and the *Panzers* had begun to roll again, driving through the eastern Ukraine towards the river Don. There were many people in Britain (including Lord Beaverbrook, Churchill's Canadian friend and the proprietor of one of the most influential newspapers, the *Daily Express*) who felt that the western Allies were not playing their full part. Something more — something significantly more — should be done to help their Russian allies.

Visiting Washington at the end of May, Stalin's emissary, Vyacheslav Molotov, was assured by President Roosevelt that there would be a Second Front in 1942, and that assurance was repeated three days later (on 1 June 1942), much to the embarrassment of the British. Winston Churchill, caught between the rock of reality and the hard place of his ally's promise, prevaricated. 'We are making preparations for a landing on the Continent in August or September

1942,' he told Molotov on 10 June, as the latter made his way back to Moscow.

> It is impossible to say in advance whether the situation will be such as to make this operation feasible when the time comes. We can therefore give no promise in the matter, but, provided that it appears sound and sensible, we shall not hesitate to put our plans into effect.

In truth, however, there was only one plan being put into effect, one for a raid rather than a Second Front, and Exercise YUKON had revealed serious weaknesses in it. YUKON II took place in 'bright, warm weather' on 23 June, both Mountbatten and Montgomery being present this time. Things went better — but not much better — than in YUKON I. More people got to the right place at the right time, although the Essex Scottish were landed late and the Camerons landed a thousand yards to the east of their assigned beach.

Nevertheless, at the end of the month Montgomery reported to Paget that he 'went over to the Isle of Wight yesterday and spent the whole day there, checking over the whole operation with Roberts, and with the Naval and RAF Force Commanders.' He continued:

> I am satisfied that the operation as planned is a possible one and has good prospects of success, given:
>
> (a) Favourable weather.
>
> (b) Average luck.

> (c) That the Navy put us [sic] ashore roughly in the right places, and at the right times....

In the event, the weather would be perfect and it can be argued that the raiders were vouchsafed 'average luck'; but in such a complex plan 'roughly' would never have been good enough in terms of time and space. How could Montgomery — a man who 'could pierce with fierce concentration into the essence of a battlefield' according to his later chief of intelligence (and Oxford don), Brigadier Edgar Williams — have been satisfied with a plan that was so overly ambitious in design and, at the same time, so inadequately rehearsed?

How could he, the great apostle of firepower, have agreed to a plan that now virtually ignored it? These are questions that have never been answered, and now never can be, but Harry Crerar — chairborne paper-chaser *par excellence* — could hardly be blamed when he, after seeing a copy of Montgomery's letter, assured McNaughton that 'the plan is sound and most carefully worked out. I should have no hesitation in tackling it, if in Roberts' place....'

Time and tides would be suitable for launching RUTTER between 4 and 8 July, and if that 'window' was not used then the raid would have to be postponed until mid-August. On 27 June General Roberts called in all his officers and briefed them on what would happen — still without mentioning the objective by name. The troops, in turn, were told of yet another exercise and, on 2 and 3 July, they were embarked on the ships and landing craft that were to carry them across the Channel. Roberts and Mountbatten visited the ships and spoke to the men; and only then was it revealed that Exercise KLONDIKE was a fiction, and that they were embarked on a raid against Dieppe.

The paratroopers scheduled to destroy or neutralize the heavy coastal defence batteries needed near-perfect conditions for their drop, however, and on 3, 4 and 5 July the weather declined to co-operate. On the evening of the 5th, the forecast for the next 48 hours was still uncertain. Moreover, intelligence suddenly announced that *10 Panzerdivision* had moved from Soissons to Amiens, only 50 miles from Dieppe. To wait until the 8th meant a two-tide raid that must extend over fifteen hours, with the withdrawal not beginning until 1700 hours — five in the afternoon — and the *Panzers* could easily reach Dieppe before that. The plan was quickly revised, placing it on a one-tide basis, with re-embarkation at 1100 hours.

It is a measure of the prevailing air of unreality and astounding over-confidence displayed on all sides that everyone concerned seems to have accepted without question a time line that suddenly called for the Calgarys and Camerons to land, fight their way inland for five miles or more, to Arques and St. Aubin, and then return and re-embark, in little more than half the time originally allotted.

An added complication came in the early morning of the 7th, when four Focke Wulf 190s on a low-level hit-and-run raid dropped two of their bombs on landing ships (LSIs) loaded with men of the Royal Regiment. The bombs were dropped from such a low height, however, that they failed to fuse themselves and passed right through the hulls without exploding, so that the Royals suffered only four minor casualties.

The men were hastily landed and preparations were under way to re-embark them in other vessels, when the meteorologists announced that the weather would still be doubtful on the 8th. So ended Operation RUTTER. 'The bitterly disappointed soldiers left their ships and the force which had spent so long in the Isle of Wight was returned to the mainland and dispersed.'

CHAPTER III

CHAPTER III

REVIVAL AND REVISION – OPERATION JUBILEE

There were now some six thousand soldiers and an indeterminate number of sailors and airmen with knowledge of an aborted Dieppe raid loose in England, mixing with other servicemen and civilians in snack bars, pubs, cinemas and private homes. Despite the continual wartime emphasis that 'Careless talk costs lives,' it was almost inevitable that some of them would talk about it — after all, it was over and done with in their minds — and that their talk would be heard, or overheard, by a considerable number of people, of whom one or more might well be spies. Prudence dictated that the project be abandoned and forgotten.

Nearly 50 years later, Volume 4 of Sir Harry Hinsley's official history of *British Intelligence in the Second World War* would tell us that 'MI 5 was virtually certain from July 1942 that all the [German] agents operating in the country were under its control.' That was very, very secret knowledge at the time, however, and for most of the officers concerned, re-mounting RUTTER was quite out of the question for reasons of security. The egregious Montgomery, for one, recommended that it be cancelled 'for all time.'

Hughes-Hallett's approach was more to Mountbatten's liking. '...the

abandonment of these two raids [BLAZING and RUTTER] was rightly felt to be tantamount to a defeat,' he recalled in 1950.

That was why so much importance was attached to re-mounting and carrying out the Dieppe raid after all... not the least remarkable feature of the operation [JUBILEE] was the fact of its having been carried out at all, and this was due to the united determination of the Chief of Combined Operations and his subordinates to drive on, unless told otherwise by superior authority.

On 10 July, only three days after RUTTER's cancellation, a COHQ meeting presided over by Mountbatten agreed that 'an alternative RUTTER should be examined,' and the next morning, according to Hughes-Hallett, 'at a meeting attended only by Mountbatten, Leigh Mallory, General Roberts and myself,' it was:

...virtually decided to re-mount the Dieppe raid with slight modifications to the plan, and carry it out on or about August 18.... Nothing was put in writing, but General Ismay [Churchill's military secretary] informed the Chiefs of Staff and the Prime Minister, who gave their verbal approval.

Thus RUTTER became JUBILEE.

At that meeting Baillie-Grohman had been notable by his absence. He had never cared much for RUTTER, being particularly concerned with what he saw as the weak intelligence background. 'This is not a criticism of the planners in any way,' he wrote, as he set about criticizing the planners. And although Baillie-Grohman wrote the critique, Roberts also signed it — two of the three Force Commanders.

(The air commander, Leigh-Mallory, a man who usually inclined to the pessimistic view, had questioned the plans for RUTTER as much as anybody, even though the air component was the least likely to come to grief. He would surely have agreed with Baillie-Grohman's critique, too, but for unknown reasons — perhaps administrative inconvenience, perhaps bureaucratic inertia, most probably political caution — he did not sign.)

Presented with these strictures, Mountbatten personally accompanied the nervous Roberts to an interview with McNaughton. According to the latter's diary, Roberts wanted to know if McNaughton still approved of the JUBILEE plan — and McNaughton gave it his blessing once again. Clearly, Roberts had his doubts, but he owed his whole career to his fellow-gunner, army commander and Canadian idol, and he was, perhaps, simply overwhelmed by two men who were both his superiors in rank and, almost certainly, in intelligence.

Baillie-Grohman presented a trickier question, to be handled by

Mountbatten in a subtler way. In a matter of days he found himself shuffled off to Admiral Sir Bertram Ramsay's staff at Dover, entirely outside of the JUBILEE 'loop' and the area of expertise that had caused him to be recalled from the Middle East in the first place. Baillie-Grohman's chief of staff, Commodore T.H. Back, also had to go. He was appointed to the command of HMS *Bermuda* — still under construction on the Clyde.

Mountbatten's next move was to ease Montgomery out of the chain of command, for he had no way of knowing that, by 7 August, Montgomery would be gone from the scene.* The CCO had a good idea, by now, of the professional insecurities that plagued McNaughton and Crerar and which were likely to make them ciphers in his hands. He proposed that a new chain of command run from Paget through them, rather than through South-East Command, thus substituting an irregular, highly sensitive, 'political' arrangement for the conventional military one. It would be a bold staff officer, or even senior commander, who would risk criticizing what might now be considered a Canadian national interest.

Flattered, no doubt, and charmed by Mountbatten, McNaughton and

---

* On the 8th he would be appointed to command of the Eighth Army and, two days later, would leave for the Western Desert and his date with destiny.

Engineers experiment with chespaling to provide traction for tanks – on a beach significantly different in texture from those at Dieppe. [NAC]

A cluster of plywood R-boats, carrying the Queen's Own Cameron Highlanders to Dieppe, mill around the Royal Navy motor launch which would lead them across the Channel. [DND]

Crerar accepted. The next day, 17 July, McNaughton took the matter up with the compliant Paget, who agreed that the formal chain of command would now run from him through the Canadians — McNaughton to Crerar and Crerar to Roberts. Since Paget's part was (by his own choice) purely nominal, there was now no experienced operational commander anywhere in the chain. Meanwhile, Churchill Mann had jumped two ranks and been appointed brigadier, general staff, of First Canadian Army on 13 July. However, Roberts asked if he might continue to work on JUBILEE until the deed was done, and his request was granted.

The prime minister and his chiefs of staff were all in favour of reviving RUTTER; and they knew, at some indeterminate but fairly early date, that Mountbatten was exploring ways of doing so, risky though it might be. They may even have known — and almost certainly guessed — that he had actually begun the process of re-mounting it. Apparently, none of them wanted to become too involved, however. In such a touchy and delicate matter decisions were anathema. As Brian Villa has pointed out, 'it seems clear that Mountbatten would have preferred to proceed with approval;' but the chiefs were having none of it.

> ...he did seek on 17 July to have the Chiefs of Staff Committee minutes record the decision to remount. Mountbatten submitted on that date a draft...to the effect that the Chiefs of Staff had ordered him to mount a substitute for the cancelled RUTTER, using the same troops...[but]...there is no indication in the minutes that the Chiefs of Staff ever acted on Mountbatten's draft minute.... Despite this, he went ahead and launched the raid.

Mountbatten had been convinced by Hughes-Hallett that the raid could be safely re-mounted and, with his buoyant and irrepressible temperament (and, perhaps, the protection of his close ties to the Royal Family), he probably calculated that if anything went wrong he could still foist the blame on to others; while, if it went right, he would be able to take most of the credit.

Those — and they will surely be many — who still find his extraordinary initiative hard to accept, might like to bear in mind the words (in his diary entry on 17 June 1944) of Lieutenant-General Sir Henry Pownall, Mountbatten's chief of staff from September 1943 to December 1944. Pownall was generally recognized as an old-fashioned officer of impeccable standards, 'a wise old head' appointed by the chief of the imperial general staff especially to keep a stringent eye on the Supreme Commander, South-East Asia.

> Mountbatten is under grave suspicion here (and with some cause) of trying to get things done under the

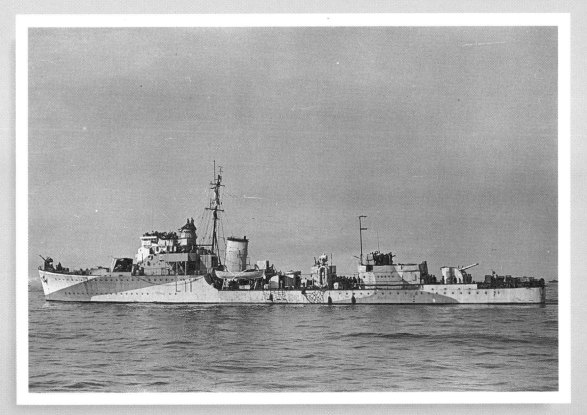

One of the eight Hunt Class destroyers whose 4-inch guns were intended
to provide fire support for the Dieppe landings. Two of them, however –
HMS Calpe, *the command ship, and* Fernie, *the alternate command ship*
– *could not make full use of their main armament since the shock of*
firing disturbed the ad hoc *radio equipment installed to maintain*
communications to the troops ashore, the aircraft overhead, and
N° 11 Group headquarters in England. [NAC]

Troops on board an Assault
Landing Craft prepare for
Operation JUBILEE. [NAC]

rose.* That was certainly a method of his when he was CCO — it was very successful and I don't doubt very necessary in order to get things done (especially with the ever-obstructive Admiralty). But however that may be, the results are the same and he is being watched [by me] very carefully for underground action. I much dislike being used for action of that kind....

Detailed planning began to amend RUTTER. If there were to be no more rehearsals, the Canadians' tasks could not be changed, except in matters of timing. The idea of a 'one-tide' raid was retained, with re-embarkarkation taking place after up to ten hours ashore, although the revised intelligence appreciation now suggested that the leading elements of *10 Panzerdivision* could reach Dieppe three hours after the alarm had been raised. In that case, the whole division could be there in six — but no one seems to have considered the implications of that.

The moon would 'set too early to be of any assistance to [their] aircraft. For this and other reasons, para troops [would] not be employed, their objectives being attacked by commandos.' The 'other reasons' included the availability of two more infantry landing ships, and by using them it would be possible to substitute commandos for parachute troops in the

assaults on the coastal batteries: N° 3 Commando at Berneval and N° 4 at Varengeville. Durnford-Slater and Lovat, their respective commanding officers, were called to Richmond Terrace, given their tasks and landing times, and left to make their own arrangements. There were now no Home Forces troops involved in the Richmond Terrace planning other than the Canadians.

The possibility of renewing the preliminary air bombardment was raised. A worried Churchill might yet, if told it was essential, see the death of French civilians as the lesser evil. Leigh-Mallory drafted a memorandum that favoured heavy bombing, proposing that it be initiated simultaneously with the flank landings.

Only half an hour is going to elapse between the landing on Blue and Green beaches [sic] instead of an hour, which was allowed in 'Rutter.' In 'Rutter' the task of the infantry landing on Blue (eastern) beach was to commence an attack on the formidable gun positions on the Eastern Cliff half an hour after they had landed, with a view to capturing these gun positions before the main landing took place.... Now, however, the frontal attack on DIEPPE will develop at the same time that the Infantry attack on the Eastern Cliff will commence. This will mean that the important defences of the Eastern Cliff must still be in action where [sic] the main attack takes place.... I feel, therefore, that some bombing of the Eastern Cliff just as the

---

* I.e., surreptitiously. The rose is an ancient symbol of secrecy.

main assault goes in will be a necessity. It is for consideration as to whether this will best be done by the diversion of Hurricane [fighter-] bombers from other tasks, or by using bombers for the purpose.

He then argued for the latter alternative, noting that the bombing 'should include a proportion of 4,000 lb bombs, so as to create the maximum destruction....' Nothing came of his proposal, however, because Churchill and Brooke had left the country at the end of July, off to Cairo first (in an attempt to sort out the organizational and operational problems that bedevilled the Middle East) and then to that 'sullen, sinister Bolshevik State [he] had once tried so hard to strangle at its birth,' to meet Stalin on 12 August.

They had left without approving an Outline Plan for JUBILEE. Drafting his memoirs, seven or eight years later, Churchill noted that 'before [he] left England for Cairo and Moscow on August 2, [he] knew that the operation was to be re-mounted.' He went on:

> Though I took no part in the planning, I was in principle favourable to an operation of this character at this time. I naturally supposed that it would be subjected to the final review of the Chiefs of Staff and Defence Committee, before whom I should certainly have had the main issues brought prior to action, had I not been abroad.

The draft was passed to Mountbatten for comment, and beside this paragraph, says Villa, Mountbatten wrote 'Please omit.' The great man obliged and left it out of volume III of his wartime memoirs, *The Hinge Of Fate.*

The decision to tighten up, by half an hour, the interval between the flank landings and those on the main beaches was more a matter of a faster-lightening sky than tactical common sense, which would have called for an earlier landing. The commandos and those bound for Blue and Green beaches would land at 0450 hours, just after the tide turned and ten minutes before sunrise, and those destined for Red and White beaches at 0510.*

Why so late ? 'First light' was at 04:30, and the 'beginning of nautical twilight' would be ten to fifteen minutes earlier than that, so that first landings timed to coincide with either would also have coincided with high tide. It was apparently because the navy feared that leaving England any earlier would increase the likelihood of *Luftwaffe* reconnaissance aircraft sighting the flotillas before dark on the 18th and raising the alarum.

Half an hour after the initial assaults, and simultaneously with the attacks on Red and White beaches, the 'exploitation' battalion — a small part

---

* All times are British Summer Time – currently in use by the Royal Navy – one hour in advance of Greenwich Mean Time, which the Germans were using, and two hours in advance of British Double Summer Time, in general use in Britain.

On a peaceful Isle of Wight beach,
battalion medics rehearse casualty
evacuation by LCA, July 1942.
[NAC]

On a peaceful Isle of Wight beach, battalion medics rehearse casualty evacuation by LCA, July 1942. [NAC]

of it borne to Dieppe in the landing craft of Able Seaman Kirby — would land at Pourville, pass through the assault force, and press inland to 'capture and destroy the aerodrome' at St. Aubin. If time permitted — remember, the raid was now a one-tide affair — it might also capture the German divisional headquarters still mistakenly believed to be at Arques-la-Bataille.

On the 20th, the chiefs of staff formally approved of Hughes-Hallet's appointment as naval force commander for 'the next large-scale raiding operation.' That has been interpreted as official approval for JUBILEE, disguised for reasons of security, but there is a good technical reason for rejecting that argument. Before finally approving any operation that came within their span of control, the chiefs needed an Outline Plan that included place and time constraints — between 'a' and 'b,' not before 'x' or after 'y' — in order that they could be sure it would not conflict with some other operation or exercise. For example, they had to be sure that a proposed raid on St. Malo would not coincide with a major naval exercise in the Channel approaches, or that one on Calais calling for heavy bomber support not be scheduled for the same night as a thousand-bomber raid on Hamburg. For this reason, if for no other, there was always an Outline Plan to be formally approved.

As for the issue of security, a simple codename such as JUBILEE was inherently more secure than a reference to the 'next large-scale raiding operation,'[*] which gave something away by the very nature of its vague language. But the 'next large-scale raiding operation' had not yet been formally established and therefore a codename could not be substituted.

All this is not to argue that the chiefs did not want RUTTER re-mounted. They, too, were under the prime ministerial gun. Sevastopol, the last Russian outpost in the Crimea, had fallen on 1 July and the *Wehrmacht* had launched a major offensive into the Donetz industrial basin — reaching the Don, from Voronezh to the Volga, by the 20th. Rostov fell on the 23rd and the Caucasian oilfields were threatened. Hitler's thoughts were turning to Stalingrad, the hinge on which the door to the Caucasus swung. Once again, it was difficult to forecast the likely depth of the German advances, or Stalin's determination to resist without more active support from the West.

Not only was there no Second Front — and, for the moment, no major raid — to distract the Germans, but from a Russian perspective Britain and the United States were failing them

---

[*] And, indeed, there was classified correspondence moving through the appropriate channels at a much lower level than that of the chiefs of staff, all appropriately labelled 'Operation Jubilee.'

In a photograph perhaps symbolic of Dieppe planning, British General Sir Bernard Paget, commander-in-chief Home Forces (extreme right), listening to another Canadian general officer, divorces himself from a discussion between General A.G.L. McNaughton [extreme left] and Major-General P.J. Montague, the senior staff officer at Overseas Headquarters. [NAC]

Troops aboard a lightly armoured Landing Craft Assault (LCA) prior to Operation JUBILEE. In the background, a Landing Ship Infantry (LSI) and a Hunt Class destroyer. [DND]

logistically as well. Convoy PQ 17, 35 merchantmen laden with war *matériel* and escorted by twenty-one warships, had sailed from Iceland, bound for Archangel, on 4 July. Nineteen of the freighters had been sunk and a hundred thousand tons of tanks, aircraft and vehicles — two-thirds of the total — lost. Such losses were not bearable. There could be no further convoys until the onset of winter, when long hours of darkness would provide an additional shield and improved prospects of getting through.

Churchill, as we have already noted, was scheduled to visit Moscow in August and it was certain that he would have to face Stalin's wrath. More than a Second Front was involved now. On 23 July the prime minister had received from the hands of the Russian ambassador a telegram complaining bitterly of the decision to suspend the Arctic convoys.

He had responded with an assurance of 'heavy raids' on the Continent in the near future but simply could not promise a Second Front. TORCH — the Anglo-American invasion of French North Africa — was going to be the major compensation offered to Stalin, but it could not be mounted before November, while the irate Russian leader was demanding something both European and immediate. Although other possibilities were under consideration, there was nothing on

Combined Operations' books sufficiently realistic and advanced to take RUTTER's place, and Churchill recognized only too well that he had 'a somewhat raw job' to do in Moscow.

Meanwhile, Hughes-Hallett arranged for the 2nd Division to be asked to produce a detailed study of lessons learned during the Isle of Wight training for RUTTER, allegedly in order that existing Combined Operations training pamphlets might be revised. That provided an excuse for concentrating a small planning staff at Combined Forces HQ, Portsmouth. Tanks had never yet been incorporated in an opposed amphibious assault, so it was logical enough for the Calgary Regiment to be asked to prepare for, and stage, a demonstration based on their training — a demonstration that would also explain away the re-waterproofing of their tanks when the time came.

The demonstration could include sappers blowing up tank obstacles and the establishment of radio communications with a hypothetical infantry force, which provided an excuse for gathering the necessary engineers and signallers once again. Finally, COHQ asked the Canadians to return promptly all engineering stores and specialized equipment (such as Sten guns and Bangalore torpedoes) issued for RUTTER. They were all stored together, to be readily available for reissue when required.

Meanwhile, the engineers were struggling with the problem of getting a Churchill tank over a two-and-a-half foot sea wall from a shifting base. Someone came up with the idea of chespaling — strips, or pales, of chestnut wood, chosen for its resilience and flexibility, linked together with wire after the fashion of snow fencing. An axle was rigged across the front of the tank and two 'bobbins' of chespaling mounted on it, one in line with each track. Then a triggering mechanism was devised which would drop the end of each length of chespaling under the tracks. As the tracks pushed the tank forward, they would pull the remainder of the chespaling down under them, providing a firm base for the 'step' up the sea wall. Hallelujah! It worked perfectly and the trial tank repeatedly rolled up and over the wall.

On the morning of 14 August its use was demonstrated to a group of officers that included the Calgary's commanding officer. That same afternoon the decision was taken to fit the device to the leading tank in each of five of the first six LCTs due to land at Dieppe. (It would be impossible to fit it on the remaining tank of the first flight, which was equipped with an experimental flamethrower that occupied the front of the hull.)

The next day five rigs were ready, and they were attached to the tanks on the 16th. It might have been better if more of the Calgary's officers had been party to these experiments, however. As it was, they were far from confident in the device when finally introduced to it, and they were given no opportunities to practice its use before setting off for Dieppe.

While these preparations for JUBILEE were going on, the troops had returned to their usual endless training — route marches, battle drills and exercises that involved live firing. The Royal Hamilton Light Infantry, for example, (commonly known to their peers as the Rileys) had practiced inter-arms co-operation in Exercise LENIN from 21 to 24 July, with tanks firing their six-pounder guns over the infantry and the usual machine-guns firing on fixed lines. Afterwards, they moved to the grounds of Arundel Castle, living under canvas and participating in a frustrating series of transport exercises, 'embussing' and 'de-bussing' and making circuits of the Sussex countryside in full battle order — all part of Hughes-Hallett's cover plan for mounting JUBILEE without arousing suspicion.

On 18 August, all the battalions embussed for what was ostensibly yet another tour of rural England, described as Exercise FORD. Instead, they were driven to the embarkation areas — Southampton, Gosport, Shoreham or Newhaven — and loaded aboard their assigned vessels. The stored equipment was reissued, and they were briefed that the raid was 'on' again.

The Royals and three rifle platoons of the Black Watch, bound for Blue Beach, boarded the *Queen Emma*, *Princess Astrid* and *Duke of Wellington* (with an appropriate sprinkling of specialists, as would be the case with the other major units); the South Saskatchewans made the passage to Green Beach in *Princess Beatrix* and *Invicta*; the Essex Scottish and RHLI were carried to Red and White beaches in *Glengyle*, *Prince Charles* and *Prince Leopold*; and the Calgary tanks (with the mortar platoon of the Black Watch) in twenty-four LCTs. The balance of the landing force was in a variety of motor launches, LCMs, LCPs and LCAs.

There were eight Hunt Class destroyers and an armada of lesser naval vessels to escort them. Two of the destroyers, *Calpe* and *Fernie* were equipped as headquarters ships with all the necessary signals gear. Too much of it, in fact, with a profusion of jury-rigged antennas interfering with each other's transmissions or receptions on key frequencies. Moreover, in an age of delicate vacuum tube technology, inadequate insulation from vibration meant that neither vessel could use its main armament without temporarily crippling its own communications, thus reducing the expedition's heaviest firepower — for what it was worth — by one quarter.

On board *Calpe* were Roberts and Hughes-Hallett, the Military and Naval Force Commanders; on board *Fernie* were their deputies, Mann and Back; while the Air Force Commander, Leigh-Mallory, would control his battle from Uxbridge, with a 'representative' on *Calpe*. Each destroyer had an air controller aboard, the one on *Calpe* being responsible for the air battle while his opposite number on *Fernie* was responsible for air support of the ground battle.

All told, there were 237 vessels in the armada that set out that night. There was some fear of mines, and according to the Combined Report on the raid, prepared in October 1942:

Before sailing the Naval Force Commander, after consulting the Chief of Combined Operations, placed on record the circumstances in which he intended to abandon the expedition. He would do so if one or more of the following losses occurred during the passage to the coast of France:

(1) HMS *Princess Beatrix* and HMS *Invicta*.

(2) HMS *Glengyle* and any other LSI with the exception of HMS *Duke of Wellington*.

(3) HMS *Prince Charles* and HMS *Prince Leopold*.

(4) HMS *Princess Astrid*.

He went on to state that, if a number of heavy Bombers could have been provided to make low-flying attacks on enemy batteries, his conclusion as to the number of losses he would accept would have been profoundly modified.

*Canadian troops practise an
amphibious landing near Seaford,
Sussex, in May 1942, on a
coastline very similar to that
around Dieppe. The pistol held by
the officer (extreme left) would be
replaced by a Sten sub-machine
gun for Operation JUBILEE. [NAC]*

All those decisions might more properly have been left to Roberts as the military commander, since such losses would affect the subsequent happenings on shore more than anything else. At the very least, they should have been promulgated as joint decisions, but by this time Hughes-Hallett seems to have taken total control of the operation.

As the night wore on, a radar station high on Beachy Head picked up traces of a German convoy steaming south along the French coast, towards Dieppè. There was nothing untoward about that: such convoys sailed two or three times a week. The radar crew, following standing orders, reported it to Admiral Sir William James' headquarters at Portsmouth, co-located with Combined Forces HQ. At 0130 hours, Portsmouth transmitted the message — in cipher, of course — to *Calpe* and *Fernie*. A little over an hour later, another warning was sent, making it clear that the two flotillas were on possible collision courses. Hughes-Hallett, to whom the signals were directed as Naval Force commander, did nothing and told no one.

Perhaps nothing needed to be done. War, as James Wolfe had observed, is an option of difficulties, and Hughes-Hallet chose the justifiable option of carrying on. What was unjustified, was apparently that he should do so without discussing the matter with Roberts, who was surely entitled to be consulted and was within a few yards

of him, at most.

It is time to turn again to Able Seaman Kirby, on board R-135.

Shortly before 0400 the sky ahead of us suddenly lit up with a myriad of tracer paths knifing into the heavens. Though momentarily startled, we were more dismayed than surprised. We all realized that we were geting close to our target, as the infantry briefing indicated a touchdown time of 0500. Now it appeared the enemy was awake and at Action Stations. Our hope of a surprise landing was dashed as we thought we were looking at German anti-aircraft fire in response to an RAF bombing raid. A few minutes later the light on the stern of R-84 began to drift off to starboard and Hop[per] had to adjust our course to 180° in order to keep her dead ahead.... Our frail wooden hull continued to be bullied through the calm French waters by our faithful Hall-Scott [engine].

What Kirby saw and heard was the northernmost column of raiders carrying Nº 3 Commando to Berneval — twenty R-boats, like his own, three having fallen out with engine trouble — coming into contact with that small German convoy making its way down the French coast, escorted by three 'armed trawlers.' The R-boats were being shepherded along by a motor launch, a Steam Gun Boat (SGB) and a Landing Craft, Flak, (LCF) — essentially a modified LCT.

Their particular escorting destroyer, *Slazak*, (a Polish ship) was about four miles away, behind the column rather than on its open flank; and its captain, for whatever reason, made no effort to intervene. Lieutenant-Colonel Durnford-Slater was aboard the SGB.

Of a sudden, star shells burst over our heads.... The shells made light out of night. I could see all our landing craft on our tail and, about half a mile away, five ships which announced their identity almost at once by pouring on us a stream of forty-millimetre and small arms fire. A destroyer had been detailed to escort us but, for the first and last time in my wartime experience, failed in her duty. She had found travelling with us at a slow ten knots too dull, and had dashed off friskily into the night. Now, when she was desperately needed, she was nowhere in reach....

The German ships teamed together most efficiently. They chose the gunboat as their principal initial target. She made a gallant effort to return the fire but, within seconds, all her armament was knocked out...

One of the naval officers was quite windy. He kept shouting:

'This is the end! This is the end!'

I was inclined to agree with him. I blew up my Mae West and undid my boots. All around me the bridge was piled up with dead and wounded like a collapsed rugger scrum. There must have been ten casualties there, all hit when looking over the top of the armour plating.... The landing craft had scattered in all directions and there was none to be seen.

Some of the German crews had identified some of the British vessels as troop-carriers, but all their transmitting antennas had been shot away during the engagement, so that they were unable to notify anyone by radio. The raiders, of course, had no way of knowing that; but it was only reasonable to suppose that German sentries on shore had seen and heard the firing, and would have sounded the alarm. Surprise should have been lost, and this was certainly the moment to cancel the raid and turn back, for the LSIs had not yet begun to disgorge their assault craft loaded with infantry — a moment in time that would mark the point of no return. But Hughes-Hallett, carrying Roberts with him, resolutely held his course.

In fact, however, although some Germans had been roused they were not taking too much notice of it. Night-time firefights between their coastal convoys and British light naval forces were not uncommon and, despite the general high level of readiness along the coast, only the garrisons at Berneval and Puys seem to have taken any action. And in the latter case, as we shall see, its additional precautions were taken more at the whim of its local commander than in calculated response to a threat.

No account of Dieppe can avoid being drawn into the question of alleged German foreknowledge of the raid. C.P. Stacey long ago established that the Dieppe defenders were not expecting this particular attack at this particular time, and his conclusion will become increasingly clear as this account of the raid progresses. More recent studies suggest, however, that while Berlin may have been forewarned, the warning was not passed down to the relevant local commanders.

There is evidence that German military intelligence (the *Abwehr*) received as many as four warnings, two of them possibly coming through 'Doublecross' agents, but took no action. That seems, on careful consideration, perfectly plausible. One can hypothesize that, knowing RUTTER had been cancelled and *not knowing* that it was being re-mounted as JUBILEE — the Inter-Services Security Board, the key agency in such delicate matters, was never told of JUBILEE, according to Professor Hinsley — it would have been a smart move on the part of the Twenty Committee to have a 'turned' agent report that a raid on Dieppe was forthcoming.

If and when the enemy then learned something of RUTTER, but not the precise date for which it had been planned, that would lead him to assume that his agent was performing effectively and thereby increase his confidence in subsequent 'disinformation' passed through him by the Twenty Committee.

On the other hand, it may be that the *Abwehr* knew, or suspected, that these particular agents had been turned against it. It also knew that there was a general state of readiness in effect all along the French coast whenever conditions of time and tide favoured a raid — a policy which, properly applied, should ensure no major surprise and severely limit the effect any such raid might have.

It would be wise, then, from Berlin's perspective, not to present the operational types with information that would subsequently prove to be false. The latter might soon come to look on such tips as a case of crying wolf, and thus be inclined to ignore unquestionably genuine warnings of more significant threats — such as invasion — when they were forthcoming. That would explain why word was not passed on, through *Oberbefehlshaber West* (*Generalfeldmarschall* Gerd von Rundstedt) and the appropriate army headquarters, to local commanders.

Similarly complex explanations can be worked out for questions surrounding the other two warnings. The problem of too many warnings, some of them contradicting others, often plagues intelligence analysts, leaving them thoroughly confused as to the truth. Intelligence services, then as now, were always endeavouring to cross, double-cross, and even triple-cross each other, after the fashion of

John Le Carré's semi-fictional spies and counterspies.

'Oh, what a tangled web we weave, When first we practice to deceive!' The simple fact remains, that whatever the Abwehr may have been told — or have believed — none of the German land, air or sea commanders involved in the defence of the Dieppe area knew that the raid was coming at all, never mind when it was to occur.

Further evidence to support this comes from the knowledge (reported by Campbell in his new book) that a SEETAKT *Kriegsmarine* radar had been removed from Pointe d'Ailly — where part of Nº 4 Commando was scheduled to land — only a week before the raid;* and that the *Luftwaffe's* FREYA radar operators on the West Headland did, in fact, pick up indications of the approaching force as early as 0230 hours (80 minutes before the convoy engagement began) only to have trouble getting anyone to take them seriously. What did the air force understand of ships and the sea? Did they realize how much night-time coastal naval and mercantile shipping activity there was in the ordinary course of events? When the airmen were able to get a reaction (from a 302ⁿᵈ *Infanteriedivision* staff officer at about 0400), it still only called for 'Increased Vigilance' rather than 'Action Stations.'

---

* More evidence that the Germans were not expecting JUBILEE. One may wonder what would have happened if RUTTER had gone ahead as scheduled and a naval warning of approaching vessels had been issued.

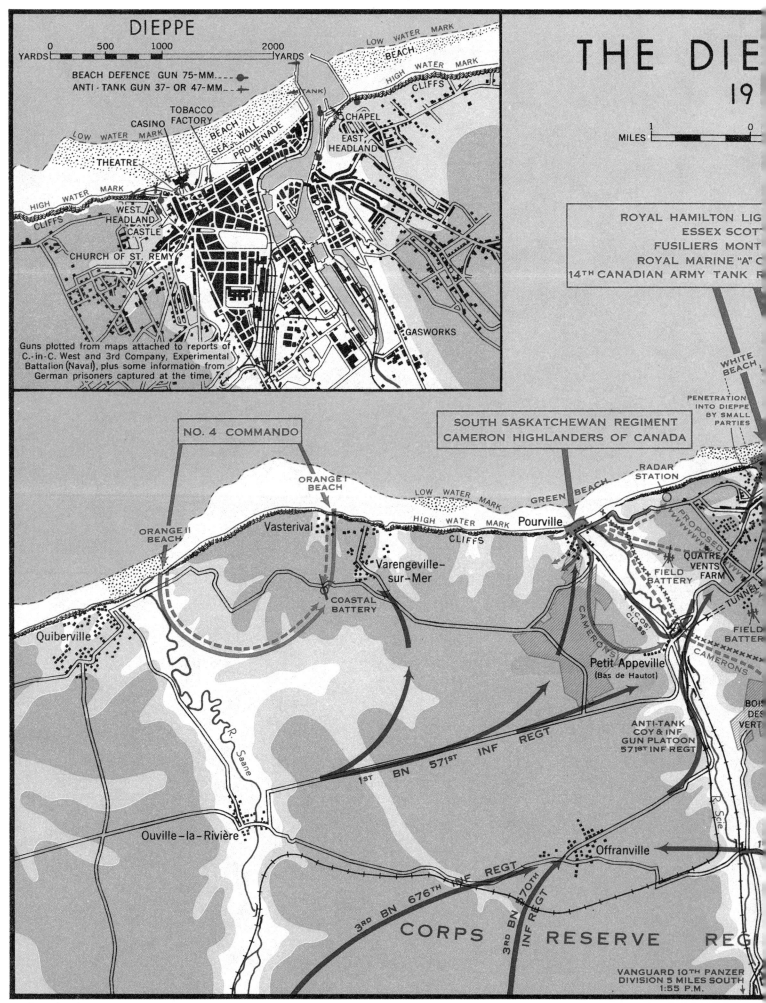

DIEPPE

YARDS 0   500   1000   2000 YARDS

BEACH DEFENCE GUN 75-MM.
ANTI-TANK GUN 37- OR 47-MM.

MILES 1   0

TOBACCO FACTORY
CASINO
BEACH
SEA WALL
PROMENADE
(TANK)
CHAPEL
EAST HEADLAND
THEATRE
HIGH WATER MARK
CLIFFS

WEST HEADLAND
CASTLE
CHURCH OF ST. REMY

GASWORKS

Guns plotted from maps attached to reports of
C.-in-C. West and 3rd Company, Experimental
Battalion (Naval), plus some information from
German prisoners captured at the time.

ROYAL HAMILTON LIG
ESSEX SCOTT
FUSILIERS MONT
ROYAL MARINE "A" C
14TH CANADIAN ARMY TANK R

WHITE BEACH

PENETRATION INTO DIEPPE BY SMALL PARTIES

NO. 4 COMMANDO

SOUTH SASKATCHEWAN REGIMENT
CAMERON HIGHLANDERS OF CANADA

RADAR STATION

ORANGE BEACH
LOW WATER MARK   GREEN BEACH
ORANGE II BEACH
Vasterival
HIGH WATER MARK
CLIFFS
Pourville
PROPOSED

Varengeville-sur-Mer
QUATRE VENTS FARM
FIELD BATTERY

Quiberville
COASTAL BATTERY
N.CO's CLASS
CAMERONS
FIELD BATTER

Petit Appeville
(Bas de Hautot)
CAMERONS

R. Saane

ANTI-TANK COY & INF GUN PLATOON 571ST INF REGT
BOIS DES VERT

1ST BN 571ST INF REGT

Ouville-la-Rivière

Offranville

3RD BN 676TH INF REGT

3RD BN 570TH INF REGT

R. Scie

CORPS   RESERVE   REG

VANGUARD 10TH PANZER DIVISION 5 MILES SOUTH 1:55 P.M.

PPE OPERATION
AUGUST 1942

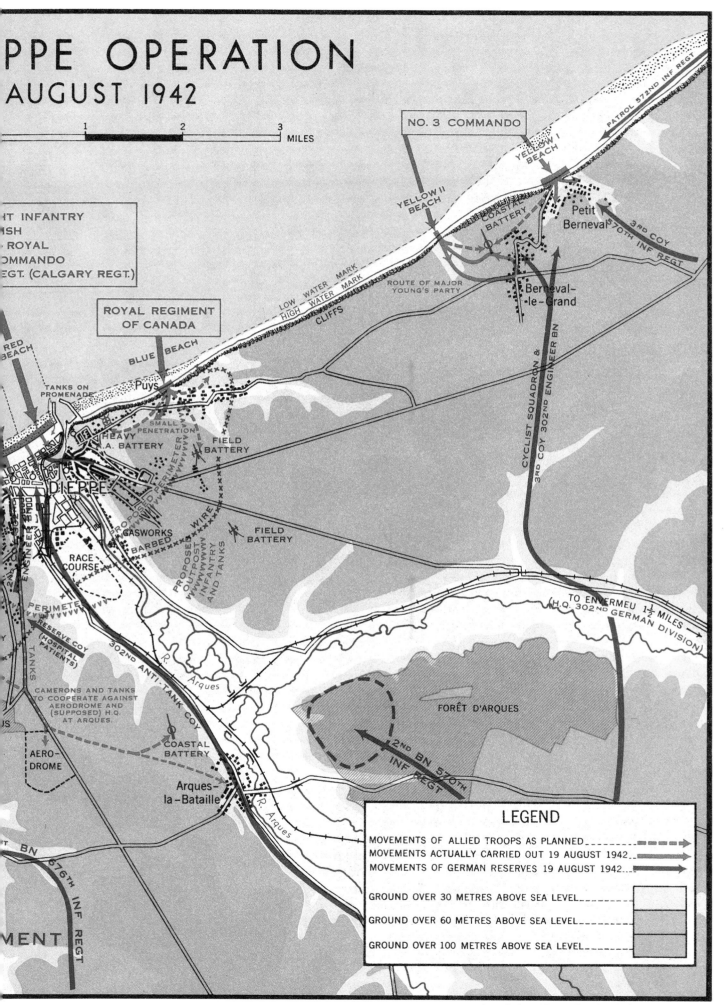

1 2 3 MILES

NO. 3 COMMANDO

YELLOW I BEACH

YELLOW II BEACH

PATROL 572ND INF REGT

COASTAL BATTERY

Petit Berneval

3RD COY 570TH INF REGT

ROUTE OF MAJOR YOUNG'S PARTY

Berneval-le-Grand

HT INFANTRY
SH
ROYAL
OMMANDO
EGT. (CALGARY REGT.)

ROYAL REGIMENT OF CANADA

LOW WATER MARK
HIGH WATER MARK
CLIFFS

BLUE BEACH

RED BEACH

Puys

TANKS ON PROMENADE

SMALL PENETRATION

HEAVY A.A. BATTERY

FIELD BATTERY

CYCLIST SQUADRON & 3RD COY 302ND ENGINEER BN

DIEPPE

PROPOSED PERIMETER
PROPOSED WIRE
PROPOSED OUTPOST
BARBED WIRE
INFANTRY AND TANKS

FIELD BATTERY

GASWORKS

RACE COURSE

TO ENVERMEU 1½ MILES
(H.Q. 302ND GERMAN DIVISION)

PERIMETE
RESERVE COY (HOSPITAL PATIENTS)

TANKS

302ND ANTI-TANK COY

R. Arques

CAMERONS AND TANKS TO COOPERATE AGAINST AERODROME AND (SUPPOSED) H.Q. AT ARQUES.

FORÊT D'ARQUES

AERO-DROME

COASTAL BATTERY

Arques-la-Bataille

R. Arques

2ND BN 570TH INF REGT

T BN 676TH INF REGT

MENT

LEGEND

MOVEMENTS OF ALLIED TROOPS AS PLANNED	- - - →
MOVEMENTS ACTUALLY CARRIED OUT 19 AUGUST 1942	→
MOVEMENTS OF GERMAN RESERVES 19 AUGUST 1942	→
GROUND OVER 30 METRES ABOVE SEA LEVEL	
GROUND OVER 60 METRES ABOVE SEA LEVEL	
GROUND OVER 100 METRES ABOVE SEA LEVEL	

Compiled and Drawn by Historical Section, G.S.

CHAPTER IV

CHAPTER IV

'A PRETTY DESPERATE STATE OF AFFAIRS'

Six of the R-boats carrying N° 3 Commando were sunk in the course of that brief but vicious firefight with the convoy escorts, and the others — many of them laden with dead and wounded — scattered in all directions. Most made their way back to England as best they could, while the crippled gunboat carrying Durnford-Slater set off to find General Roberts, aboard the command ship, HMS *Calpe*.

Five of the LCPs which had been at the head of the column held their course for France, however, four of them (led by Motor Launch 346 which subsequently engaged a small German tanker and drove it ashore) reaching Yellow I Beach at Petit Berneval and the fifth ending up beneath a cleft in the cliffs, a half-mile to the west, that constituted Yellow II. The 'Goebbels' battery of four 155-mm guns lay on the headland between the two landing sites.

Those bound for Yellow I touched down 25 minutes late, at 0515 hours.* In the clear light of dawn, two machine-gun posts covering the beach

were ready and waiting for them. Both were quickly taken, but before they were silenced a number of men had been killed or wounded and Ranger Lieutenant Edwin Loustalot had become the first American killed in European land warfare during the Second World War. The message reporting this landing took an hour and a quarter to reach *Oberbefehlshaber West*, outside Paris, and it apparently constituted that headquarters' first notification of the onset of JUBILEE.

There were other strongpoints in the valley leading up to Berneval, their garrisons aroused by the firefight at sea. The survivors of some seventy men who had landed began to push inland but were too few to make much impression on an alert, well-armed and well-protected enemy; indeed, they were soon in desperate straits, with half their number dead. The plywood, unarmoured R-boats that might have evacuated them were held off by German fire and only one man was able to swim out to a landing craft and thus return to England. The others, every one of them wounded, were taken prisoner.

From Yellow II, however, the swashbuckling Major Peter Young (who had won a Military Cross at

---

* Readers are reminded that all times are British Summer Time, (one hour in advance of Greenwich Mean Time, that being the time used by the Royal Navy, under the rubric of 'B' Time) and not Double British Summer Time (used by the rest of Britain) or GMT (used by the Germans).

Vaagsö) and his twenty men climbed the wire-choked gully undetected and set out to neutralize the German battery — even if they could not destroy it — after cutting the telephone wires that linked Berneval to Dieppe. Circling around behind the gun positions, they opened fire with rifles and light machine-guns from a range of two hundred yards, and for three hours they continued to snipe away, harassing the enemy so effectively that the demoralized gun crews could only manage an occasional, fruitless, shot at the ships soon circling off Dieppe.

After three hours (which was a longer stay than wisdom might have suggested) Young and his troopers made their way back to the beach, where their boat was waiting, re-embarked, and sailed back to England. By the time that the commandos left, the Germans at Petit Berneval were too disorganized to shoot any better in their absence than they had done while under fire. Young and Lieutenant H.T. Buckee, RNVR, the commander of the R-boat, were made members of the Distinguished Service Order for their gallant work, two of the earliest of the 133 decorations eventually awarded to those who participated in Operation JUBILEE.

At the western extremity of the raid, carried from the LSI *Prince Albert* by LCAs, 252 men of Lovat's Nº 4 Commando landed unopposed on two beaches. One troop, seventy strong, scrambled ashore three minutes late at Vasterival (Orange I), almost directly in front of the 'Hess' battery's six guns and 112-man garrison on the edge of the hamlet of Varengeville. The others landed exactly on time, at 0450 hours, at Quiberville (Orange II) nearly three miles to the west. This larger group, meeting no opposition,* trotted inland nearly a mile, along the valley of the Saane, and then struck off across country, to approach the battery from the rear.

The Vasterival party opened fire with mortars and machine-guns at 0550 hours, keeping the German gunners fully occupied while the Quiberville group got into position. Twenty minutes later, in the course of a pre-planned air strike on the battery, a bomb or cannon shell struck the Germans' 'immediate' ammunition reserves, which promptly blew up with a 'blinding flash.' (The commandos believed that it was one of their mortar bombs that caused the explosion, but German sources attribute it to aerial attack.)

At 0620 the firing of a Very flare launched simultaneous charges on the battery position by both commando groups** and hand-to-hand fighting

---

* Although someone must have seen them, since various German headquarters subsequently received reports of a landing at Quiberville. In the alternate initial scenario for RUTTER, it will be recollected, this was where the tanks were to have landed.

** One being led by Captain P.A. Porteous, RA, who was wounded three times and was subsequently awarded a Victoria Cross.

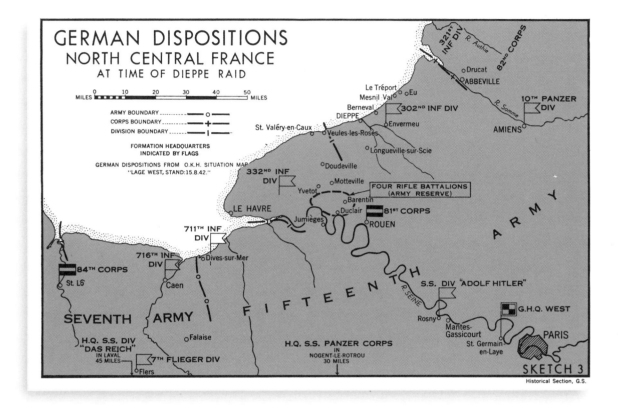

GERMAN DISPOSITIONS
NORTH CENTRAL FRANCE
AT TIME OF DIEPPE RAID

MILES 0   10   20   30   40   50   MILES

ARMY BOUNDARY .... —•—
CORPS BOUNDARY .... —+—
DIVISION BOUNDARY .... —|—

FORMATION HEADQUARTERS
INDICATED BY FLAGS

GERMAN DISPOSITIONS FROM O.K.H. SITUATION MAP
"LAGE WEST, STAND:15.8.42."

321ST INF DIV
R. Authie
82ND CORPS
Drucat
ABBEVILLE
10TH PANZER DIV
R. Somme
AMIENS

Le Tréport
Mesnil Val
Eu
302ND INF DIV
Berneval
DIEPPE
Envermeu
St. Valéry-en-Caux
Veules-les-Roses
Longueville-sur-Scie
Doudeville
332ND INF DIV
Motteville
FOUR RIFLE BATTALIONS (ARMY RESERVE)
Yvetot
Barentin
LE HAVRE
Duclair
81ST CORPS
Jumièges
ROUEN
ARMY

711TH INF DIV
716TH INF DIV
Dives-sur-Mer
FIFTEENTH

84TH CORPS
St. Lô
Caen
R. SEINE
S.S. DIV "ADOLF HITLER"
G.H.Q. WEST

SEVENTH   ARMY
Rosny
Mantes-Gassicourt
St. Germain-en-Laye
PARIS

Falaise
H.Q. S.S. DIV "DAS REICH" IN LAVAL 45 MILES
7TH FLIEGER DIV
Flers
H.Q. S.S. PANZER CORPS IN NOGENT-LE-ROTROU 30 MILES

SKETCH 3
Historical Section, G.S.

resulted in heavy casualties on both sides. Among the Germans there were:

> *...30 killed, 21 wounded recovered by own units, among them gravely wounded troop commander; at present [2010 hours] 10 missing, of these the majority probably have been recovered as wounded by relieving troops.... A telephone operator in the telephone bunker did not allow himself to be overrun, held bunker alone until relieved, threw back a hand grenade which was thrown in, is now badly wounded and in hospital. Guns damaged by blowing and partly burned out.*

The bulk of N° 4 Commando then left via ORANGE I beach, 46 of their comrades having been killed or wounded, or gone missing.

Despite the miscues and misfortunes of war, and the imposition of heavy casualties, one commando attack had achieved a total, and the other a substantial, degree of success — successes that could be attributed to careful planning by men who knew what they were about; some achievement of surprise; and a lavish distribution of initiative, improvisation and courage. Now it was the Canadians' turn.

Hauptmann Richard Schnösenberg, commanding the battalion that was responsible for defending Dieppe Ost — Puys, the Eastern Headland, and half the inland perimeter (for the Germans practised 'all-around defence') had had his men up for much of the night, carrying out his own private exercise in Increased Vigilance. He had just released all but the normal sentries, and returned his command to the usual dawn alert status, when the official call for Increased Vigilance was issued as a result of the convoy battle. Since no one was likely to be asleep as yet, it was just as convenient to turn his whole battalion out again.

That was what he did. Most of its positions were on the headland (looking out over Dieppe) and the inland perimeter, however, and Puys (which was much smaller then than now, consisting of less than twenty houses) was defended by only two platoons — one army and one *Luftwaffe* — and some miscellaneous technical troops, numbering 'probably well under a hundred men in all.'

The beach that they were responsible for was only some two hundred yards long, overlooked on both sides by sharply-rising cliffs; and on the steep flanks of each, two 'pill-boxes' had been sited so as to cover the foreshore between them with enfilade fire. For about two-thirds of its length that foreshore ended in a buttressed ten-foot-high sea wall and, as the Royals' regimental history observes, 'all in all, it would have been difficult to discover, anywhere on the coast of Europe, a less favourable area for an assault landing.'

The landing craft assigned to carry the Royal Regiment to shore from the

A Royal Navy motor launch escorts LCTs towards Dieppe.
A net hangs over the side of the launch to ease the problem of heavily
laden soldiers trying to embark or disembark. [NAC]

The western end of Blue Beach (Puys) in 1942. 'All in all, it would have
been difficult to discover, anywhere on the coast of Europe, a less
favourable area for an assault landing.' Colonel Catto and his party
scrambled up the hillside somewhere on the right of this picture. [DND]

LSIs *Queen Emma* and *Princess Astrid* fumbled the forming-up procedure and, as a result, approached the shore in three quite separate waves — the first of them about twenty minutes late, at 0510 hours, when it was already light. An 'informal enquiry,' held aboard *Queen Emma* two days later, attempted to make sense of what followed.

Lieutenant-Commander H.W. Goulding, RNR, the specialist navigator who was responsible for guiding the first wave of seven LCAs (from *Princess Astrid*) into Blue Beach, assessed the initial opposition that they met as *'light machine gun fire.'* Goulding had been in action before and already had a DS0, awarded for 'good service on enemy coasts,' so he probably knew what he was talking about. He added that, *'Major [G.P.] Scholfield got off promptly with a couple of men. The rest had to be urged.'*

The officer in charge of the flotilla, Lieutenant W.C. Hewitt, RNVR, explained exactly how they were 'urged' in a written report.

When about 100 yards from the beach, light machine gun fire with armour-piercing bullets was encountered, and also infilade [sic] fire from the right hand pill box. Major Scholfield, the senior army officer, and the boat officer in my craft were both wounded, the fire coming from half-way up the gully down into the boat.

When the soldiers started to jump on to the beach everything opened up. A number of casualties occurred before the troops reached the shelter of the wall. This discouraged the rest from landing and only a firm handling of the situation by the naval officers in charge of each landing craft succeeded in compelling the rest to follow their comrades, revolvers having to be used as a threat.

Hewitt expanded on part of this in his verbal testimony at the enquiry.

Q[uestion]. Can you describe landing?

A[nswer]. *When about a hundred yards away we came into line of fire of light machine guns, bullets of which penetrated boats. We suffered some casualties. I then asked Bren gunner to return fire. This he did very wildly and fired into the bows of the boat.*

Q. Was there any damage done ?

A. *Yes. The runner of the door [ramp] was damaged thus jamming the door. Major Scholfield cleared jam and was first out of boat.*

Q. What was attitude of soldiers ?

A. *Soldiers appeared reluctant to leave boats and were forced out by Lt.Cdr. Goulding and myself. Those who landed ran straight to the wall but did not attempt to climb. They left two scaling ladders in boat. At this time there was heavy firing from pill-boxes.*

A second wave of landing craft — from *Queen Emma* — closed the shore fifteen or twenty minutes after the first.

Notre Dame de Bon Secours chapel, on the Eastern Headland overlooking the port. The bunker beneath, clearly visible in this photograph, offered a clear field of fire across Red and White Beaches. [DND]

Another view of the beach at Puys, taken in 1944. The beach obstacles so clearly visible in this photograph were not there in August 1942. [DND]

Two of them were *'cleared immediately'* of their passengers, according to naval testimony, but several others brought in more men reluctant to disembark into the inferno of fire that awaited them. Lieutenant E.C.W. Cook, RNVR, for one, reported that *'they were reluctant to leave boat and had to be forcibly made to disembark. There were a number of wounded in boat. They left the mortar apparatus behind in boat, but did eventually get it off.'*

What did it look like from a willing soldier's perspective? *'People had shot over us and around us [during training],'* recalled one officer in the second wave, *'but nobody had ever shot at us — and there's a big difference, a very big difference.... As I left the assault craft I saw perhaps a hundred dead men.'* The psychological shock would have been severe, even for men accustomed to battle; for neophytes, it was brutal.

Sergeant J.E. Legate was also *'in the second wave to land and when [he] hit the beach the battle was really in shape.'*

> *When I got off [the LCA] the dead and wounded were lying all over the place. The machine gun fire coming from the Germans deadly beyond getting anywhere to take up a fire line on them ourselves [sic]. We just had to stay close to the wall that was there. The cross fire coming at us made it impossible to move two feet from the wall or you got it. There was nobody around to look after the wounded and if there was [sic] it was impossible to get near them. The Germans by this time were getting the range with their mortars, and the shells were dropping all around us, and by this time again it was impossible to give orders to try and do anything and it turned out to be every man for himself. That was the battle as I saw it.*

Last of all came the LCAs from *Duke of Wellington*, manned largely by Canadian sailors and carrying 110 officers and men of the Black Watch of Canada. Only a little more than half of the highlanders landed, however, close under the cliff to the east of the beach and, happily, largely out of reach of the German machine-gunners. Only four were killed and eight wounded, two of the latter and all the unwounded being subsequently taken prisoner.

On the beach in front of the wall, scaling ladders were raised by a few brave men and a number of Bangalore torpedoes were exploded in the wire, to little or no avail. A mortar crew 'set up a 3-inch mortar on the shingle and managed to fire three bombs before they were cut down by machine-gun fire,' but on Blue Beach prodigious bravery was mostly a passport to quick death. Late in the battle — if it can be called that — about 25 men *'suffering losses, scrambled through the wire entanglements reinforced with mine charges,'* according to a German after-action report, which added,

The Dieppe esplanade, viewed from the side of the chateau, half-way up the West Headland, shortly after the Raid. A 4-inch shell appears to have penetrated a tower of the Chateau (and the conical roof has been knocked in), while one wing of the Casino and one of the temporary buildings erected on the esplanade by the Germans can be distinguished on the left, in the middle distance. [DND]

Red and White Beaches, seen from a bunker on the East Cliff, below Notre Dame de Bon Secours. [DND]

brusquely, that *'they were annihilated at 0815 hours....'*

Two or three men seem to have got over the wall and through its accompanying coils of barbed wire via a recessed flight of steps at the western end of it. Only one, Lance-Corporal L.G. Ellis (who was subsequently awarded the Distinguished Service Medal), managed to get back again, after wandering about the village on his own for perhaps an hour before being wounded in the head, arm and leg by a mine.

Towards the eastern end of the beach, at the point where the sea wall ended and the chalk cliff of the Eastern Headland began, a small re-entrant, blocked by barbed wire, gave some cover from the deadly enfilade fire. A considerable but uncertain number of Royals, including their commanding officer, Lieutenant-Colonel Douglas Catto and his artillery Forward Observation Officer, Captain G.A. Browne, RCA, (both of whom would subsequently be awarded DSOs) gathered there.*

There were no Bangalore torpedoes conveniently to hand on this part of the beach, so they created a gap with manually-operated wire cutters. Shortly after 0600 hours, some twenty men, Catto and Browne among them, were making their way up a narrow angle in the cliff which provided some shelter from the enemy's fire. Moments later, however, machine-gun fire emanating from a new enemy position covered the hole they had cut in the wire.

'We discovered that we could not get back to the beach,' Browne reported, in a 1943 interrogation after his escape from the Germans. *'Nor could we get back to the cliff edge because of L[ight] M[achine] G[un] fire from the left flank, up on the hill-side.'* They cleared two houses, meeting *'resistance'* in one, but only *'a shot or two from the other.'*

Just at this moment, Lieut. Ryerson saw a strong patrol coming along the road through the trees towards us from the direction of the fortified house on the left flank.

The decision was made to move...along the cliff top by the walled road under cover of the trees as far as they went. We would try and contact the Essex [Scottish]. Accordingly, we struck through the small wood immediately to the WEST and above the beach, towards N[otre] D[ame] de BON SECOURS.

Moving in that direction and then finding Germans all around them, they had little option but to hide in a convenient copse, having worked

---

* Browne's radio operator had survived the initial landing and had been transmitting messages to Roberts, aboard *Calpe* (via another destroyer, HMS *Garth*) outlining the desperate predicament on Blue Beach. None of them, however, seem to have reached Roberts in the form in which they had been sent. The first arrived at 0620 and was recorded as 'R Regt C not landed.' Twenty minutes later, Roberts still believed that the battalion was not ashore, when he ordered it to land at Red Beach to support the Essex Scottish.

German soldiers man a slit trench on the landward side of the Dieppe esplanade. In the background (extreme left, below the West Headland), the Casino is still standing, suggesting that the picture was taken before 19 August 1942. [ECP Armées]

Soldiers of the Toronto Scottish regiment man an anti-aircraft machine-gun aboard a Tank Landing Craft bound for Dieppe. [NAC]

themselves into the strongest part of Schnösenberg's defences.

Why did they go that way ? The Eastern Headland had been the Royals' primary objective all along, but its tactical importance was such that commonsense should have suggested twenty men could not take it; and that there would be little prospect of joining up with the Essex Scottish, who (even had their own landing been successful) would still have been separated from them by harbour channels and basins that ran inland for more than a mile before becoming the river Arques.

On the other hand, had they attacked and overcome that 'strong patrol' coming towards them (or even dodged it), twenty men with the advantage of surprise might well have cleared one or more of the fortified houses at Puys and, at the very least, sufficiently distracted the remaining defenders to have enabled some of their surviving comrades to get off the beach.

That, of course, is easier to say now than it would have been to do then, in the harsh reality of battle with reason blanketed by the fog of war. But one wonders what Peter Young and his 20 commandos would have done in the same situation? It was surely a case in which previous experience of combat would have been an invaluable aid to decision making. Browne's account continued:

A scout of our party who went out on the road to [do a] rec[onnaissan]ce was shot. The Germans had LMGs sited at each road and track intersection in this vicinity, with fields of fire in all directions. Shortly after ten o'clock (or it may have been nearer eleven) while in the wood, we heard the survivors of the beach being marched past under guard. Before noon it was apparent that, for all the sound of firing we could hear both from RED and WHITE beaches, as well as BLUE where there was none, there was little or no land fighting, and that the operation had resolved itself into an air battle.... The 88 mm [Flak] battery of 6 guns on the cliff top between N[otre] D[ame] de BON SECOURS and PUITS [Puys] served its guns magnificently. It was low-level bombed at least four times and machine-gunned oftener by our fighters after 1000 hours, with us as witnesses....

Twice we made a recce to the cliff edge to see what might be taking place at DIEPPE, but we could see neither the beach, which was just barely out of sight around the bend in the cliffs, nor any sign of ships. The situation suggested that we were trapped. After long consideration the decision was taken to surrender. We surrendered at 1620 hrs.

On the other side of Dieppe, at Pourville, the first wave of landing craft carrying the South Saskatchewan Regiment from the LSIs *Princess Beatrix* and *Invicta* reached the shore on time without a shot being fired.

Dead Canadians still litter the beach in this photograph, looking across
Red Beach to the harbour entrance. In the foreground, a largely-
undamaged Landing Craft Assault; behind it, a burning
Landing Craft Tank. [ECP Armées]

Looking west on White Beach from a position in front of the Casino, with
the West Headland to the left of the tank turret and the cliffs beyond
Pourville to the right of it. Tanks which had reached the esplanade
returned to the beach to act as immobile bullet-proof shelters offering
some slight protection to the foot soldiers trapped there. [ECP Armées]

Green Beach was much longer than Blue — perhaps six hundred yards from end to end — and the sea wall rather lower, but still eight feet high in places. Almost in the centre — and certainly further to the west than it is now, in its currently channelled form — the Scie made its leisurely exit into the English Channel through a set of sluices.

At the Dieppe end of Green Beach, a steep cliff rose to become the Western Headland (with the radar station on top of it); and at the other end, a somewhat lower, but still substantial, cliff chopped off a wooded ridge that ran inland, forming the western edge of the valley of the Scie. Half of the SSRs should have been landed east of the river, close under the Dieppe headland, from where they could quickly push inland, hook around, and assault the radar station's defences from the gentler slope of the landward side.

Nearly all them were landed west of the river. Happily, however, the lack of initial opposition did enable them to cross the sea wall quickly, and for the most part easily. Turning to their left, those bound for the radar station and Dieppe then had to work their way through the village (again, much smaller then than now) and cross the Scie before approaching their immediate objectives.

The weight of enemy fire began to build up rapidly. Some men waded the swampy creek that was the Scie immediately above the sluices,* using the road bridge that spanned it as cover. Others tried to rush across the bridge only to be mown down by machine-gun and mortar fire from the high ground beyond; and here their commanding officer, Lieutenant-Colonel Cecil Merritt, won the first of two Canadian VCs granted for Dieppe. He *'led several parties across the bridge...which was swept by machine gun, mortar and f[iel]d gun fire continually,'* reported Captain H.B. Carswell. *'On many occasions he crossed over the bridge... The men followed him splendidly, but were shot down time after time.'*

Those who got across the Scie, one way or another, were faced with an intricate network of mutually supporting mortar and machine-gun fire. Using fire and movement tactics, some of them tried to edge up towards the barbed wire fences that ringed the radar station, only to come under enfilade fire from the vicinity of Quatre Vents farm, further inland. One was Sergeant W.A. Richardson.

The range was about 550 yards but enemy fire was extremely accurate.... A plan of attack was laid out, but as we could not contact Navy for support barrage on the hill on our right [towards Quatre Vents farm], it was dropped, as it was impossible to cover

---

* Below the sluices, it was 'a tiny trickle running out of a six-foot brick drain above high water mark.'

Looking east on Red Beach, a wounded Canadian can see the bodies of his comrades awaiting removal. The broken track on the tank was more likely the result of a German shell than a French pebble. [ECP Armées]

As the tide rises, German intelligence specialists search the turret and driving compartment of this tank for documents (maps, orders, maintenance manuals, etc.) which might be useful to the enemy. Two copies of the Operation Order were taken ashore and fell into German hands. [ECP Armées]

so much open ground without supporting weapons.

...Capt. Osten and approximately 25 O[ther] R[ank]s attempted to advance up the slope on the left but were driven back by heavy mortar fire....

While good fighters at long range, the enemy showed no inclination to counter-attack, although he seemed to be in a good position to cut off our withdrawal if he showed initiative and guts.

Having once got across the Scie the SSRs were not incurring horrendous casualties, even though they were unable to reach their objectives. The Germans, of course, professionals to their fingertips, would have been foolish to launch counter-attacks, since they were heavily outnumbered. Better to defend their fortified positions, for now. The raiders were being held off, and there was no real need for counter-attacks. If they should eventually be needed, let such potentially costly manoeuvres wait on the arrival of reinforcements.

On the far side of Pourville, 'C' Company of the South Saskatchewans was enjoying more success. N° 14 Platoon had lost nearly half its strength while still aboard the LSI *Invicta,* when a mishandled grenade had exploded while being fused; but as the platoon sergeant pointed out, *'the fact that we only had 16 men left in the platoon did not worry Mr. [Lieutenant] Kempton'* — his young platoon commander.

We picked up a few prisoners but as Mr. Kempton was set on getting to the objective he turned the prisoners over to another platoon and kept going.

On nearing the objective Mr. Kempton insisted on going ahead alone and looking it over before allowing us to attack as...due to our shortage of men he did not want to run us into trouble by carrying out the plan we had originally laid down. Coming back, he re-organized the plan of attack and led the charge in himself.... The attack was successful due to his wonderful leadership and the determination of the men to follow him wherever he went.

After we had consolidated, Mr. Kempton took a few of the men out in front of our position and searched farm buildings on our right and left flanks for enemy snipers.... He then reported to the O[fficer] C[ommanding] the Co[mpan]y as to our successes.

At approximately 0945 hours a lone car was seen coming down the road into town which we had covered, but Mr. Kempton was not to be fooled by it and did not give orders to fire on it. It soon turned around and went back the way it had come and disappeared into the bush about 2,000 yards away. Soon we were able to see the enemy moving out of the trees, and a section started down the road in our direction followed shortly afterwards by larger bodies of troops. We allowed them to get into range and [then] opened fire with all we had, taking our toll of them before they had a chance to get to cover on the sides of the road.

They moved back to the cover of the trees again and proceeded to pull a

Perhaps the most famous of all Dieppe photographs; but captions rarely mention that the body second from the bottom of the picture is that of a US Army ranger, judging by his American-style gaiters.
[ECP Armées]

With one arm still raised in fatal agony, a badly burned body lies on the barbed wire-strewn shingle of Red Beach. In life, this soldier was most probably a sapper whose backpack of high explosive was set alight by enemy fire; the Germans had no flamethrowers in action at Dieppe.
[ECP Armées]

pincer on us.* Mr. Kempton said to me, 'Now we are in a hell of a fix as our flanks are unprotected except for what fire we can produce ourselves. I hate to keep the boys [here] but we will have to stick it [out] until they get in on top of us and then make the best [we can] of getting out as they are relying on us in the town.' He sent word back to Coy. HQ telling of our position and proceeded to arrange things for the withdrawal when the time comes [sic].

The experience of 14 Platoon is recorded in such detail because it is a wonderful illustration of a platoon commander meeting all the responsibilities of a junior officer. But, despite the gruesome loss of half their number in a pre-raid accident, the initial introduction to battle of these lucky Canadians was as moderate as could be expected, and far less harsh than that inflicted on the Royals at Puys. With excellent leadership such as that provided by Kempton, they gave as good or better than they got.

Half an hour behind the South Saskatchewans, the Queen's Own Cameron Highlanders — who, like Durnford-Slater's commandos, had come all the way across the Channel in their little R-boats — came into Green Beach. Closing the shore, the coxwain of R-135, Able Seaman Kirby, relinquished the helm to his deckhand, and prepared to ignite the smoke generator on his boat's stern.

The water ahead of us began to erupt like a massive sea volcano as a rain of mortar fire descended upon the water in front of us. Smoke billowed from our generator and piled up behind us in great clouds that obscured everything in that direction. Plowing through the wall of mortar fire, the noise was deafening. But more than that, the concussion of each burst pressed on our ears as though we were being smitten with giant pillows.... I am half soaked from the water cascading down on me as I crouch down behind the smoke generator....

I see the Cameron platoon commander pointing off to his right. Looking in that direction I am amazed at the sight of a piper standing up on the focs'le of the second boat over, playing away as though he was alone in a field of heather.... Shortly before touching the beach, the din is joined [sic] by the staccato chorus of a number of automatic weapons from the cliffs that spring from either side of the stoney beach in front of us.

The roar, the crash, the rattle and smash, have reached such a crescendo that it fairly blocks out my ability to appreciate what is taking place around me.

Even as the Camerons jumped from their boats, their comanding officer, Lieutenant-Colonel Alfred Gostling, was killed by a bullet in the head, for the beach was now under fire from the Western Headland. *'No specific Coy. tasks had been assigned, as it was considered there might be some confusion on landing*

---

* I.e., began to outflank them on both sides.

This man probably died with his boots on: but where were they when this photograph was taken? His waterbottle, helmet and gas mask are still to be seen. [DND]

Surrounded by the litter of war, and with his face covered with field dressings, a wounded man aboard an LCA waits for medical help. [ECP Armées]

and that it would be better to allow the individual Coy. commanders to meet whatever situation might arise' — an interesting contrast to the preliminary planning of Lovat's commandos, for example, among whom, 'because of the prearranged plan for seating in the LCAs no reorganization was necessary on landing.'

There was, indeed, 'some confusion on landing', this battalion being beached astride the Scie (as the SSRs should have been) instead of entirely to the west of it, as planned. Naturally enough, given their lack of specific tasks, those who landed east of the river ended up *'in close contact with Col. Merritt and fought under his orders,'* rather than driving on towards their own battalion's objectives. In other circumstances, such extemporization might have turned a well-planned success into disaster, but on this day disaster was enthroned in its own right.

The Camerons were supposed to make their way to Arques-la-Bataille and St. Aubin along the east bank of the Scie, but because there was no clear way across the river in or near Pourville, the remainder of the battalion, under its former second-in-command and new commanding officer, Major A.T. Law, set off up the west bank, harassed by long-range fire from the Quatre Vents area but meeting no really serious opposition. Had a squadron of tanks been landed with them, at Pourville, however —

perhaps the squadron that never landed on Red and White Beaches — it might have helped the SSRs to take the radar station and enabled the Camerons to move a good deal faster.

Reaching Petit-Appeville, a mile and a half inland from Pourville, there was still no sign of the tanks that were supposed to link up with them; and, since *'time was getting short,'* — there had never been enough time for this expedition, once the raid had been shortened from a two-tide to a one-tide operation — Law now decided to abandon the original plan, cross the river by the Petit-Appeville bridge, and *'secure the high ground beyond,'* on which the Quatre Vents farm stood. However:

> *Enemy troops were now seen advancing across the high ground at LE PLESSIS. About the same time a horse-drawn mortar detachment was knocked out by 'A' Company as it approached the bridge from the south. Three enemy close-support infantry guns, also horse-drawn, arriving by the same route, succeeded in crossing the bridge and took up positions covering it. These guns were engaged by small-arms fire but without effect, being well shielded.*

Law concluded that there was no chance of forcing a way over the bridge — that the stream was fordable at many places seems to have occurred to no one — and, at about 09:30 hours, he issued orders to retreat to Pourville. No sooner had he done so than he received a radio message announcing

This tank reached the esplanade but apparently slipped sideways into some kind of pit – or perhaps a trench system – and was unable to get out. [ECP Armées]

Standing among a number of bodies, a German officer wearing the ribbon of the Iron Cross speaks to two men who may be Canadian prisoners while a German soldier, hands on hips, surveys the damage. [ECP Armées]

the forthcoming early evacuation from the beaches; and minutes before he did so, *10 Panzerdivision*, at Amiens, had reported that its vanguard would be ready to move at 0945, with the main body to follow at 1100 hours.

During all these adventures on the right flank, Flight Sergeant Nissenthal and his escort had apparently got quite close to the radar station, and cut some cables leading to it, but like everybody else they were unable to enter the perimeter. There is no evidence that their participation had any impact on the radar war. *Wrong! Read The book "Green Beach" by James Leasor*

'In war,' said Napoleon, 'even the simplest thing is difficult.' Ideally, perhaps, all the landings should have been made simultaneously, at the beginning of nautical twilight, thus ensuring surprise all around. But the number of vessels involved, their wide range of speeds and sea-keeping qualities, and the inevitable congestion that would have resulted from all trying to put their men ashore at the same time, had led the navy to veto that for RUTTER and the prohibition had carried over to JUBILEE. The landings must be staggered.

Thus, if all had gone according to plan, the Royals and the South Saskatchewans would have been in possession of the cliffs that dominated Dieppe's main beach by the time that the RHLI, Essex Scottish, and Calgary tanks reached it. But even if the opposition at Puys and Pourville had been weaker than it was and the Canadians bolder, even if surprise had been achieved and the friction of war been minimal, knowledgeable planners would have allocated (and experienced raiders demanded) a full hour for the two flanking forces to achieve those objectives, as had been stipulated in the original plan for RUTTER. The half-hour allowed by the JUBILEE planners was absurdly short.

As it was, neither of the flanking forces had come close to achieving their objectives in the stipulated time and the frontal assault now faced a thoroughly aroused enemy emplaced in ideal positions to scythe down advancing infantry — the only moderating factors being a pre-arranged attack by cannon-armed Hurricanes on the buildings lining the esplanade, while a pair of Bostons laid smoke over the headlands. The Hurricanes were there for less than five minutes and the smoke blew away inland about as fast as it was laid.

Red and White Beaches, between them, extended for almost a mile, while the distance between the two headlands was slightly more, the East Cliff being separated from Red Beach by the harbour entrance. The sea wall was much lower here than at Puys or Pourville — two to two and a half feet — and behind it a largely unobstructed

The Y-shaped exhaust stacks, fitted to enable the tanks to plough through five feet of water, are prominent in this photograph; although the much larger but less robust air intakes have all disappeared. [ECP Armées]

It seems that when their right-hand track was broken, after reaching the esplanade, this tank crew swivelled their tank through 180° so that the armour protected them while they escaped through the still-open side hatch. A spindle for the chespaling on the front of the tank, and the waterproofed air intakes and exhaust system on the back, are still intact. [ECP Armées]

esplanade, about 120 yards wide, ran back to the buildings that lined the landward side of the Boulevard Foch.

On White Beach (the western end), a well-fortified neo-classical Casino complex protruded across the esplanade, almost to the sea wall. Just to the east of it a couple of temporary huts had been constructed (which gave some 'cover from view,' if not protection from fire), and some minor trench systems had been dug in places that provided the Germans with tenuous, mostly unmanned, outposts on the esplanade.

Strongpoints on and in the cliffs offered incomparable fields of fire across the beaches and the esplanade. The East Cliff (on which stood the chapel of Notre Dame de Bon Secours) was the most heavily fortified and armed of the two, its garrison bearing the chief responsibility for guarding the harbour entrance. At ranges varying from three hundred to fifteen hundred yards, machine-guns, light artillery of various calibres and mortars had absolutely clear fields of fire over 90 percent of Red Beach and the esplanade behind it.

The infantry came in on time, at 0520 hours, but the first of the LCTs carrying the Calgary tanks were 'about ten or fifteen minutes late in touching down.' Would their prompt arrival have given the infantry that increased confidence (and practical support from their 2- and 6-pounder high-velocity guns and co-axial machine-guns) needed to 'rush' the esplanade? It seems unlikely, but who can say with certainty what might have happened in other circumstances.

'There was a momentary lull in the firing as we touched down, then it opened up again with terrific intensity...' recalled the RHLI's Lieutenant-Colonel Robert Labatt, in a report originally prepared in a German prison camp and smuggled out by an officer who was repatriated on medical grounds in 1944. *'We doubled up the beach some 25 yds, then dropped flat.'*

The protective pl[atoon] [commanded by Captain W.D. Whitaker] *was fanned out and my signallers were with me. I reported to B[riga]de we were ashore, then looked around. The right Co[mpan]y was having a bad time. Two of their boats had been hit and were washing listlessly against the beach. 20 yds ahead the centre Coy was getting through the wire. The left Coy and the SX [Essex] had landed and were crossing the beach.*

Every German emplacement on the cliff, in the Casino, on the Mole and along the sea wall was going full blast. 50 yds away a terrific fight was going on for the Casino pillboxes.

In a slight hollow in the shingle, Labatt established his battalion headquarters, but there was little he could do. As he observed in his report, *'It was still very much a Coy and Pl Com[man]ders fight....'* Somewhat later, Brigadier Lett, unable

The wounded awaiting succour and the dead awaiting burial are intermingled on White Beach. [ECP Armées]

Lying among their dead comrades, wounded Canadians wait for relief on Red Beach. [ECP Armées]

to land from an LCT which had been badly damaged while landing its tanks, was severely wounded (and most of his little tactical headquarters party likewise killed or wounded). His 4th Brigade command therefore fell upon Labatt, as the senior battalion commander, but the appointment was largely meaningless.

A quick appreciation revealed a pretty desperate state of affairs.... My right Coy had been practically annihilated before reaching the wire and its survivors were pinned to little hollows in the beaches. In the centre we had got through the wire, captured the Casino and small parties were in the town. This operation had been costly and had used up most of the centre and reserve companies. The left Coy had got through to the esplanade, there to be practically wiped out. Its survivors had moved to the right, joining up with the units around the Casino.... The beach was a deathtrap, laced by MG fire from 4 directions* and by mortar and shellfire from 3.

The Casino proved to contain a maze of corridors, alcoves and small rooms, as well as the main gaming rooms, and desperate hand-to-hand fighting developed, with the Canadians eventually taking some twenty German prisoners — not all of whom were finally brought off from the beaches. Some of these prisoners, at least — and others in other places — had their hands bound together in order to make them easier to control, despite a provision of the Geneva Convention which specifically forbade such treatment.*

A group of about 14 Rileys succeeded in getting into the town through the Casino.

Captain [A.C.] Hill led us over the courtyard and up to the Regina Hotel. Machine-gun fire was heavy and I even saw the tracers passing in front of us. We went through the hotel to the cinema, and then up a narrow street. The sniping was bad [for us]. We couldn't see the flash of the rifles and we couldn't locate them. Some women waved to us as we went by and one civilian was waving with one hand with a pistol in the other. We killed him with rifle fire. Near the church we ran into a group of enemy and CSM Stewart dispersed them with the Bren gun fired from the hip.

They roamed the streets around the Église St. Remy for the best part of an hour, sporadically exchanging fire with startled Germans to no great effect on either side. Then they holed up in a theatre just behind the Casino for about two hours, until it became clear

---

* A machine-gun at the end of the harbour mole was firing at the beaches from the rear.

* Commandos customarily tied up their prisoners, for obvious reasons, much to Hitler's annoyance. Shortly after Dieppe, he retaliated by ordering that all commando and Dieppe prisoners of war be shackled. On a tit-for-tat principle, the British government then shackled an equivalent number of German prisoners and tried to persuade the Canadian government to follow suit. To their credit, the Cabinet declined, and gradually the shackling of Canadians was abandoned by the Germans.

Lying entangled in the barbed wire, this soldier appears to have had one leg blown off. Somone tried to dress the wound, then abandoned a hopeless task. [DND]

that there would be no significant reinforcement. Finally, with German soldiers 'converging on the theatre from more than one direction,' they sprinted back to the Casino. Hill got a Military Cross for his gallantry, and Stewart a DCM.

A little later, Lance-Sergeant G.A. Hickson of the Royal Canadian Engineers (whose assignment had been to destroy the Dieppe telephone exchange, but who had been caught up in the fight for the Casino as it became clear that the exchange was beyond reach) organized another group of Rileys and fellow sappers to make a foray into the town. They, too, were beset by enemy snipers.

The men were much surprised to find that, in spite of this, a number of civilians, or at any rate persons in civilian clothes, were moving freely about the streets and making no attempt to take cover. After watching the situation carefully for some time, our men came to the conclusion that these 'civilians' were, in fact, giving away the positions of individual Canadian soldiers to the enemy snipers; they therefore cleared the streets with Bren gun fire.... One house was cleared and the party of German infantry holding it destroyed. There was hand-to-hand fighting in this house. Ammunition becoming exhausted...before retiring they did all possible damage, including cutting telephone cables. While on their way back to the Casino, they heard the hooter signal for withdrawal.

Hickson's was another well-deserved DCM.

The Essex Scottish lacked even that little cover provided by the Casino. Looming over them was the East Cliff, and in front stretched 120 yards of open esplanade on the other side of a wired sea wall. This was where, to quote again US General George Marshall's instructions to Colonel Truscott, 'there could be no substitute for actual battle in preparing men psychologically to meet the nervous tensions and uncertainties of combat.'

Their only hope of success — indeed, the only hope for survival of many of them — would have been to cross the esplanade at once, taking what casualties they must; but many of them were simply stunned into immobility by the awesome impact of intense battle — the deafening noise of mortar bombs bursting on shingle, the staccato bursts of machine-gun fire, the howl of aircraft engines stressed to the limit, the sharp, unending bark of field, anti-tank and anti-aircraft guns, and the groans and screams of their wounded comrades.

There were brave men among them. According to Captain D.F. McRae, an attached officer of the Stormont, Dundas and Glengarry Highlanders, *'the Essex Scottish returned the fire over the sea wall and made at least three stubborn attempts to cross the wall, each time being badly cut up by gunfire and machine-gun fire.'* The

A hole ripped in its side and much damage done to its superstructure, a Tank Landing Craft still burns the day after the battle. [ECP Armées]

bravest, however, were soon killed or severely wounded, as had been the case on Blue Beach — *'The mortar detachment fired on their objective until destroyed by shell-fire.'* McRae also noted that the initial casualties *'were attended to as far as possible by stretcher-bearers and uninjured troops.'* Harsh as it may seem, those lucky enough to have escaped injury in disembarking should have been focussed on crossing the esplanade, not succouring their wounded comrades.

As always, there were notable exceptions. Company Sergeant-Major Cornelius Stapleton, commanding an ad hoc platoon of cooks and drivers told to 'protect' battalion headquarters, had stepped ashore dryshod, from an assault landing craft that had not been touched during the approach. Stapleton had been away from the battalion, on a detached posting, for the past two months and had missed all that intensive training on the Isle of Wight; but he knew instinctively that the beach was no place to be or stay.

Gathering up nine or ten of his men, he charged a weak point in the wire, where it had just been partially cut and flattened by the Germans' own mortaring, and led them through it and across the esplanade without anybody getting hurt.

I lay it 90 percent to good luck, and the fact that we were in the very centre [of the beaches], which you would think [sic] *that everybody on the hills [cliffs] could very easily have concentrated on us; but they were so busy with what was going on in front of them, that they weren't.... probably the way they should have been.*

In another group that also tried to cross just a little later, seven out of nine were hit, the two unhurt men subsequently joining up with Stapleton in the town. No doubt, luck played a part in both cases, but had every unwounded man tried to do the same, more or less simultaneously, perhaps half — or even three-quarters — of them might have reached the boulevard in good health, for the enemy fire would have been diffused accordingly.

Stapleton and his men worked their way through the intervening streets to the buildings lining the outer harbour.

We spotted a little tug-type ship coming up [the harbour channel] and tying up at the wall, over on the opposite side, with quite a few naval personnel on it. Our fellows wanted to open fire. I said, 'Wait 'till they tie up, get them standing still....' They tied up — they had to go ten, fifteen feet up the ladder over the sea [harbour] wall — so they started to climb up there and I said, 'Now,' and we just poured everything to them. We couldn't tell from that distance how many actual casualties there were, or whether they were just diving for cover....

Demonstrating a rare combination of courage and judgement under pressure, Stapleton took many risks but none of them were foolish or

avoidable ones. Few men have done more to deserve the DSM that he was subsequently awarded. Moving back into the old town, between the harbour and the esplanade, he saw:

...an old gentlemen at a window on the second floor...pointing down the street, warning us that there was something there. So we got very cautious and we peeked around the corner and there's a truck in front of the building and the Germans...getting on the truck.... So we waited for them. I don't know how many men around the truck—I believe I saw about six or eight run from the building and get on the truck, then the last one got on and the truck started to go.

Started gliding right towards us, so I said, 'Fire now, let her go!' We had maybe eight or ten good bursts of machine-gun fire on that truck. [It] came to a stop (the headlights came on — why I don't know) and there was considerable hollering but nobody got out of the truck.

There were other firefights. Picking their targets, shooting and being shot at, Stapleton and his men wandered about the town, *'house hopping down to the area where we were supposed to meet regimental headquarters and the other [protective] platoon.*

By this time it was getting close to ten-thirty/quarter to eleven. I decided, 'there's no use being caught here; if we're going to start taking off we might as well get back to the beach,' and we started working our way through the buildings and never really ran into any enemy contact at all. Working our way through, we were very cautious where we were going, jumping from one building to another.

When we did get back to the hotel [through which we had entered the town] again, we got out in the yard [bordering the esplanade] and the bombardment was still going on, but there were a few Calgary tanks rolling up and down the thing. We were afraid that if we made a move they'd fire at us. I had one guy take his shirt off, wave it, signal, get some attention — all we got was a blast of machine-gun fire....

There was a lull in the mortar fire when we went across the promenade [but] there was some rifle fire at us.... When I said 'Go!' and took off, I know three or four men came with me and others may have straggled [after us], but two men were lost from that point on. Now whether they were lost going across the promenade, or whether they got back to the beach and were taken out there, I don't know.

We were probably fired at, but we just took off. That's the only way we could go — just took off, went across the wall, took a high dive over the wire and on to the beach.

The tanks should have landed simultaneously with the infantry, but the first of them were fifteen minutes late — fifteen very important minutes — and some of them, as we shall see, soon lost another fifteen minutes simply through their crews' lack of foresight. The LCTs of the first wave carried miscellaneous troops — signallers, brigade staffs, intelligence

The streets leading back into the town from the esplanade were blocked with concrete. One such barrier can be seen on the left of this picture of German soldiers walking past discarded Canadian helmets. [DND]

A petty officer of the Kriegsmarine examines Lieutenant Edwin Bennett's tank, 'Bellicose', after the battle.

officers, photographers — as well as three tanks each. In one of them was Major B. Sucharov, inventor of the chespaling device and the officer commanding the engineers' beach parties.

N° 1 Tank moved off on touchdown, stalled on [LCTs] ramp about 5 minutes due to motor not having been warmed up. This tank had track-laying device. It then proceeded up beach to esplanade wall, laid its track, climbed wall, turned right on B[ou]l[e]v[ar]d, jettisoned the apparatus and proceeded in Westerly direction. The other tanks were observed to follow tracks of first and similarly surmount esplanade. Each tank stalled on ramp and 15 minutes elapsed before all three tanks were clear of LCT.

On the other hand, the tank carrying Lieutenant-Colonel Andrews was too quick to leave its LCT.

At approximately 100 yards from the beach, the Sub-Lieutenant who was forward gave orders for the ramp to be lowered half-way. The foremost tank, seeing the ramp being lowered... rushed forward, hit the ramp, parted the lowering wires and disappeared over the bows into the sea — the T[ank] L[anding] C[raft] passing over it.

Andrews survived the sinking but was killed while struggling ashore.

The shingle itself, Sucharov reported, cost only four tanks broken tracks, although a number of others subsequently lost theirs as a result of artillery and mortar fire. Major C.E. Page, the senior Calgary officer to

reach shore, *'did not see or hear of any of the tanks using the chespaling attached to the front. In most cases it fell off or was knocked off. It had been fitted very hurriedly....'*

The tanks that landed near the centre of Red (Essex Scottish) Beach found that their way to the esplanade was barred in places by an artificial ditch immediately below the sea wall. This unexpected impediment was the result of German engineers excavating shingle to mix with concrete in the construction of their strongpoints and road blocks, but it acted as an effective anti-tank obstacle. Those tanks which tried to negotiate the ditch quickly became stuck fast when they nosed down into it.

Lieutenant Edwin Bennett, approaching the shore in the second wave of LCTs, had already been burned about the face and hands and caught metal splinters in his right eye, after the landing craft carrying his troop of tanks was hit shortly before reaching shore.

When we saw the tanks [that had landed before us] stranded, I decided that we would stick to the waterline and go along until we could see a place where we could go over the sea wall, but it was quite something going along the beach because of all the bodies. The ones we encountered I would say were in pretty bad shape and there were places where we had to straddle or go around them.

N° 6 Brigade headquarters had been aboard the same LCT as Bennett, and

The bodies had been removed from Red Beach and apparently French civilians were free to study the scene by the time that this photograph was taken. Both the scout cars allocated to the two brigadiers can be seen – one at the water's edge, the other half-buried in shingle in front of the one remaining tank. [ECP Armées]

A Churchill tank that reached the esplanade before having one track blown off by German gunfire. [ECP Armées]

Brigadier Southam followed him ashore, into the chaos and confusion. He could no more get a grip on the battle than his wounded fellow brigadier or Colonel Labatt.

> Soon after this I saw my 19 [radio] set and went to help get it across the beach. We suddenly realized we were about to be run down by a Churchill — moving quickly from East to West. We waved at it and attempted vainly to move the 19 set from its path; some fast jumping saved us from being bumped, but the 19 set was not so fortunate.... Soon after this I found Major Rolfe operating a W[ireless]/ T[elephony] radio] set in the remains of a scout car which he stated had been run over by one of our tanks.... We did contact 4 Bde at one time and Brigadier Mann at another time.

Bennett had now passed the end of the excavation and swung his tank round to climb the shingle.

> ...the sea wall was not as high in front of the Casino.... I asked Bobby, the driver, to go up there but go slow and steady, and we just gradually crept up and finally we were on the esplanade....
>
> We went along the boulevard in front of the buildings and every entrance [into the town] was blocked by a concrete road block about three to three and a half feet high...but we went all along the full length of the boulevard and cleared the Germans out of the trenches....
>
> We moved along the esplanade, back and forth, back and forth, right from the Casino to the harbour. Even the road leading along the harbour area was blocked off with the concrete blocks which our engineers were supposed to blow. They had no opportunity whatsoever to reach that far ashore....

A total of 29 tanks, out of 58 embarked, went off the LCTs; and, of the 27 that landed, 15 crossed the sea wall. None of them could get beyond the esplanade, all the entrances off the Boulevard Foch being closed by massive concrete road-blocks that proved impervious to the tanks' own fire.

Sappers bearing great packs of high-explosive and the necessary fusing on their backs had been assigned to blow the concrete away. On foot, and unshielded, most of them had already been killed or wounded, however,* (as were most infantry radio operators) and none of the survivors could get near their objectives. There was nothing wrong with the Churchills' armour, however. Most of the German anti-tank guns were of 37-mm calibre (with a few of 57-mm) and during the whole of the battle only two tanks were holed, one in the rear and one in the side. None were set on fire by the enemy and, as far as can be ascertained, none of the crewmen were injured while inside their tanks.

Hovering offshore were the landing craft carrying General Roberts' reserve

---

* Engineer casualties were proportionately highest of all at Dieppe.

*One of the Hunt Class destroyers
laying a smokescreen to protect
landing craft leaving the Dieppe
beaches. In the event, smoke
proved far more valuable than the
fire of its 4-inch guns. [DND]*

— Les Fusiliers Mont-Royal and the Royal Marine Commando. Radio communication with those on the beaches was poor and uncertain all morning and, on occasion, it did more harm than good. This was one such occasion. Somebody transmitted a signal to *Calpe* that 'some of the Essex Scottish are in the town' but the first three words had been dropped from the text by the time it reached Roberts — who knew by now that the assault on Blue Beach had been a total failure.

The only Scottish in the town were those in Stapleton's small party, but Roberts understood that most — or at least a substantial part — of the battalion was there, and that was good news. Success on Red Beach might yet compensate to some extent for the disaster on Blue. He promptly ordered the Mont-Royals to land behind the highlanders ; but, since the shore was largely obscured by smoke and the heaviest fire was coming from the East Cliff, naval coxwains unwittingly and instinctively edged away from it. Most of the Montrealers were put ashore on White Beach instead, and almost half were trapped on a narrow strip of shingle right under the West Cliff, where they could accomplish nothing. One of them, Lieutenant A.A. Masson, found that his men *'seemed extremely bewildered by the turn events had taken.'*

The remainder found themselves deposited in front of the Casino, where some of them joined up with the Rileys who were occupying it. Sergeant-Major Lucien Dumais found himself there, *'among the wounded and dead who lay scattered on the beach.'*

Some of the wounded were trying to swim out to the boats [and] many were bleeding heavily, reddening the water around them. [Once ashore] mortar bombs are bursting on the shingle and making little clouds which seem to punctuate the deafening din... Close to me, badly mutilated bodies lie here and there. The wounded scream...the blood flows from their wounds in a viscous, blackish tide... For myself, I am absolutely astounded to have reached my shelter in one piece. I was certain that my last hour had arrived.

Sergeant Pierre Dubuc was another soldier in the Stapleton mould. Finding a tank that had been 'drowned' in landing but was now exposed by the falling tide, (was this Colonel Andrews' tank ?), he and another soldier climbed in and *'fired away the whole of its two-pounder ammunition at the German positions on the cliff.'*

Abandoning the tank and picking up a Bren light machine-gun, he then rallied a dozen men and started into the town from the back of the Casino. They made their way through to the inner basin of the harbour, killing and wounding a number of Germans on the way, but were compelled to surrender when they ran out of ammunition. Their weapons and clothes were taken from them (but their hands were not bound) and they were left in the care of one unfortunate young guard who took his eyes off them for one brief but fatal moment. Dubuc jumped at him and brought him down, while another soldier snatched up a piece of pipe that lay to hand, and *'swinging it over his head, cut the German's head in half.'* The Canadians then scattered, wearing only their underpants, and Dubuc made his way back to the beach alone. He was another winner of the DCM.

'I went [back] down to the shore and, in spite of the hell going on there, managed to gather a few able-bodied men,' recalled Lucien Dumais. *I wondered why we were not all dead: it should not have been possible to pass through such a hail of bullets without being hit.'* With what men he could muster, he returned to the Casino and tried to push ahead, into the town, without success. A little later:

> *Of my 45 men, only four were still with me, that was all. The others were scattered all over the place. A good number of them were still on the beach, dead or wounded, or possibly some of them were pretending to be....*
>
> *Formations no longer existed. Soldiers were rubbing shoulders with men who were not only from other companies, but from other battalions, even from other branches of the service. There were sappers from the engineers, tank crews, dispatch personnel and many others. It was a hotch-potch:....*
> *We were in a vicious circle and the situation was getting worse by the minute.*

Another misleading signal, accurate enough in itself if taken literally, told General Roberts at 0815 hours that the Canadians '[had] control of White beach.' Still in reserve were the men of the Royal Marine Commando, lurking behind the offshore smokescreen, and a desperate Roberts now ordered them in behind the Rileys with instructions to 'pass around the West and South of the town, and attack the batteries on the Eastern cliff from the South.'

Such an instruction suggests that he was now losing whatever grip he might once have had on the situation. It would have required, at the very minimum, a penetration of two and a half miles or more through the streets of the town (where no one had yet managed much more than two hundred and fifty yards), including crossing the inner harbour bridge — certain to be well-guarded — and a climb to the heavily-defended high ground beyond.

Some of the tanks still afloat were ordered to land in support, but that was cancelled ten minutes later. The commandos started for shore but came under heavy fire as soon as they cleared the smokescreen. As his boat beached, their commanding officer, showing immense physical and moral courage as well as impeccable judgement, stood up on the bow and signalled his men to turn back from an impossible task. He was mortally wounded seconds later, but all but three of the boats — which, like his, had already reached shore — turned back into the smoke.

By 0900 hours it was clear to everybody concerned that, except for the two commando attacks on the outer flanks, JUBILEE was a fiasco, if not a catastrophe. Roberts and Hughes-Hallett, anxious, now, to limit the slaughter on the beaches, agreed at 0930 hours that a general withdrawal should begin an hour later — it would take that long to be sure that the word to evacuate had been passed to all concerned. And Roberts wisely set that timing back by a further half-hour on being advised by Air Commodore A.T. Cole, Leigh-Mallory's representative on *Calpe*, that the extra half-hour would ensure additional air support.

CHAPTER V

CHAPTER V

SALVAGING THE DAY

The air battle had been more successful than the ground one, even though it had not been the triumph that the Air Staff had hoped for.

Focussed, as it was, entirely on air superiority — which was admittedly a prerequisite of any other projection of airpower — aggressive support of ground forces held little interest for the RAF at this time. Perhaps that was why 56 fighter squadrons were (rightly) committed to JUBILEE, but only two squadrons of fighter-bombers, two of tactical reconnaissance machines, five of light bombers — and two of USAAF B-17 heavy bombers.

Reviewing the raid shortly afterwards, the German commander-in-chief in the west thought that 'the employment of the enemy air force and their tactics were extraordinary.'

It seems incomprehensible why, at the beginning of the enemy landings, the Dieppe bridgehead* and other landing places were not isolated by a continuous curtain of bombs, so as to prevent, or at least delay, the employment of local reserves.

The RAF order of battle included 48 Spitfire squadrons, all intended to ensure air superiority — which was, and is, the prerequisite of effective ground support. With 16 aircraft in each, to a total of 768 machines, numbers alone were clearly on the RAF's side, although only four squadrons were equipped with the new Spitfire IX* — the technological equal of the Focke Wulf 190 that provided the bulk of the *Luftwaffe's* air superiority force in the west. Six of the Spitfire squadrons were Canadian — N°ˢ 401 and 402 with Spitfire IXs, and N°ˢ 403, 411, 412 and 416 with VBs.

Their opponents mustered less than two hundred serviceable fighters (mostly Focke Wulf 190s) and 120 bombers (mostly Dornier 217s, and only about half of them serviceable on 19 August) within useful range of Dieppe. The RAF/RCAF flew over two thousand fighter sorties, the *Luftwaffe*, about six hundred; the RAF nearly three hundred bomber sorties, and the Germans 125.

---

* Because of the scale of the raid and the employment of armour, he was under the initial impression that, had the assault been successful, a prolonged or permanent occupation was intended.

* So new that, had RUTTER gone ahead, there would have only been one squadron of Spitfire IXs available.

Six squadrons — nearly a hundred machines — were hovering overhead when the landings began, but they were hardly needed. The first Focke Wulfs did not put in an appearance for an hour, since the pilots of *Jagdgeschwader* 26 at Abbeville, the nearest German fighter base, had been partying the night before — more evidence that the local Germans had not received notice of the raid.

When they did appear, it was some time before there were more than a dozen of them. British and Canadian airmen remarked on the reluctance of the enemy to press home attacks but, given the disparity in numbers, one can easily understand why. Later in the day, when there were German bombers to be protected, they were more than willing to engage the RAF/RCAF fighters. The bombers, easily visible in their black night camouflage paint when they began to arrive in mid-morning, concentrated their attention on the shipping since there was clearly no need for their services on shore.

N° 412 Squadron's Flight Lieutenant J.M. Godfrey, who arrived on the scene shortly after 0600 hours, reported that:

> Over Dieppe it had been impossible to keep the squadron together and everybody split up into twos. The sky was filled with a swirling mass of Spitfires and FW 190s milling around.... Everybody had a squirt [of machine-gun fire] at about three

Jerries, but it was impossible to see the results, because as soon as a pilot squirted he could be sure a Jerry was on his tail and had immediately to take evasive action. We were much encouraged when all our boys returned safely.

On a later sortie:

> There were FW 190s all over the place around 2,000 feet, and we were the only Spits at our height. Some 190s started to dive down on the Hurri[can]es [attacking gun positions on the ground]. We tore after them and they, seeing us coming, started to break away. Just then, someone yelled, 'Red Section, break.' There were some 190s on our tail[s].
>
> We went into a steep turn to the right and shook them off. I lost the others for a few seconds. The Flak started to come up at us in great volume. Red balls [of fire] were shooting past my nose uncomfortably close. I spotted my N° 1 and joined him. Just then, the C[ommanding] O[fficer] yelled, 'Let's get out of here.'
>
> We dove down onto the sea, going all out and weaving as hard as we could. The Hurries were about two miles out to sea, on the way home. We managed to keep the Jerries busy, so that none of them had been attacked. We stayed with them on the way home, weaving around them with our heads turning about 120 [times] to the minute, looking for Huns. However, none chased us back and we landed with the whole squadron intact.

Godfrey and his comrades were lucky to escape intact on that occasion,

His mind focussed on the question of air superiority, in mid-1942 Air Vice-Marshal Trafford Leigh-Mallory, CB, DSO, the Air Officer Commanding of Fighter Command's N° 11 Group and Air Commander for JUBILEE, had little concern for the complexities of air/ground co-operation. [IWM]

19 August 1942 was a warm day, and Second World War battledress was not the most appropriate costume. Fear is thirst-making, as well as tiring, and no doubt these Canadians were glad to get a bucket of fresh water. [ECP Armées]

'The plan is sound and most carefully worked out...,' wrote Lieutenant-General H.D.G. Crerar, General Officer Commanding, I Canadian Corps, an enthusiastic seeker of combat for Canadian soldiers. Here, in an October 1942 photograph, he poses with his brigadier, General Staff, Brigadier Churchill Mann, who had been the staff officer responsible for the detailed planning of Dieppe. [DND]

as they did throughout the day, while the intensity of the air battle varied, with never less than three RAF/RCAF fighter squadrons on the scene and nearly always four or more.

Before nightfall, Leigh-Mallory would lose 99 aircraft, most of them fighters, with Canadian losses accounting for 13 (nine pilots, one a prisoner of war) of that total. At the time, his airmen claimed to have destroyed 91 enemy aircraft (with 38 'probables' and 140 'damaged'), although the actual figure was 48 — 25 bombers, 23 fighters — with another 24 damaged. The Royal Navy lost only one destroyer (the *Berkeley*) and a proportion of the 33 landing craft sunk by air action, with two more destroyers (including *Calpe*) and other lesser vessels damaged.

But if, by and large, allied airmen prevented the enemy from injuring their comrades, as von Rundstedt noted they did very little to injure the enemy. In terms of pre-planned support, the first bombers — two Bostons each from Nos 107 and 605 Squadrons, RAF, and 418 Squadron, RCAF, set out to bomb the coastal defence batteries at Berneval and Varengeville at 0445 hours — five minutes before the commandos assigned to take them were due to land. One of the Canadian machines was compelled to return with engine trouble and the other was shot down, although the crew was saved; none of

them came even close to hitting their targets.

Half an hour later, more Bostons and Hurricane fighter-bombers attacked the batteries again; and this time it is possible that major damage was inflicted at Varengeville when charges stacked beside the guns were blown up by some projectile. The commandos attributed the explosion to their mortar fire, but German accounts blame low-flying enemy aircraft.

If the Germans were right, then it certainly marked the airmens' greatest success of the day in terms of contributing to the ground battle. As the RHLI and Essex Scottish closed the shore, and Bostons laid smoke over the headlands in an effort to mask the approaching boats, five squadrons of cannon-armed fighters blasted their way along the length of the esplanade. However, their stay was necessarily brief, the weight of fire they delivered light, and they did little damage. An after-action report rightly observed that 'we might have achieved more by using the cannon fighters and Hurri-bombers against the 6-inch [coastal defence] batteries, and the [bomb-dropping] Bostons for the attack of houses on the front at low level.'

The German positions on, and in, the flanking headlands could have been totally destroyed, had the Admiralty not been so pusillanimous about risking a battleship in the Channel. Fourteen- or 15-inch guns,

Lance-Corporal L.G. Ellis of the Royal Regiment of Canada won his Military Medal on Blue Beach, where he 'displayed the greatest initiative, skill and devotion to duty.' [From an oil painting by Lawren Harris – National Gallery of Canada]

'A daring and cool-headed soldier,' Sergeant Pierre Dubuc of Les Fusiliers Mont-Royal won his Military Medal for leading a small group of soldiers into Dieppe and subsequently escaping from captivity. [From an oil painting by Lawren Harris – National Gallery of Canada]

using conventional and bombardment charges, as appropriate,* could have brought great masses of chalk crashing down about the cave entrances while wreaking havoc on the reinforced concrete of the bunkers built on top. The buildings lining the landward side of the esplanade, sheltering snipers and machine-gunners, could very easily have been reduced to rubble. The relatively puny 4-inch guns of the destroyers, however, no matter how boldly served, could do none of those things. Lieutenant F. Royal, an official photographer on board an LCT that did not land its tanks, recorded how *'one of the most impressive sights that was witnessed was at approximately 0930 hours. A small destroyer* [Albrighton] *came past us and moved into the mouth of Dieppe harbour and opened fire.... It fired salvo after salvo for about forty-five minutes'* — but he might have added that it had little or no impact on the headland to judge by the weight of fire that continued to fall on the immobile Essex Scottish.

Worse was to come. In a foul-up over impromptu support reminiscent of that at Vaagsö, lessons laboriously learned by Army Co-operation Command through trial and error over the past two years were simply not applied by Fighter Command, which had total charge of the air effort. Army Co-op had developed a fairly sophisticated system of control designed to respond quickly to the often unpredictable demands of ground combat and to discriminate effectively between multiple demands. Leigh-Mallory, however, preferred to rely on an ad hoc system that ran from units or formation headquarters on the beach, through a controller on *Calpe** to Uxbridge, then from Uxbridge to the appropriate sector station, from the sector station to the relevant airfield, and from the airfield to the squadron.

As a result, there was a time lag of one and a half to two hours between a request for support being transmitted (when an operator could get through, which was not always the case) and aircraft arriving over the target (when they found the right target, which was also not always the case). To give one example, at 1144 hours, while the evacuation was in full swing, a request from Brigadier Southam for more bombing of the headlands was only met (with Hurribombers and cannon-fighters) at 1330 hours — after most of those troops still on shore, including Southam, had surrendered.

---

* Bombardment, or reduced charges gave a ship's guns the trajectories of howitzers, so that, at a sacrifice of range and penetration, shells could be lobbed with relative accuracy on to a land target. Using regular charges, if a shot was a fraction high it would whistle inland for miles, far beyond the range where it might have done any good, but shells dispatched in that fashion, with the correct elevation, would also have penetrated the soft chalk of the vertical cliff face before exploding.

---

* Another controller on board the alternate command ship, *Fernie,* handled the air superiority battle: both came under the command of Air Commodore Cole, on *Calpe.*

Squadron Leader Lloyd Chadburn, DFC, the commanding officer of N° 416 Squadron, RCAF, leans against the wing of his Spitfire V, with, behind him on the fuselage of his machine, the squadron emblem – a charging lynx superimposed on a maple leaf. Chadburn won his DFC for leadership at Dieppe. He would add a DSO and Bar to his decorations before dying of injuries incurred in a crash in June 1944, a week after D-Day. [NAC]

As commanding officer of the South Saskatchewan Regiment, Lieutenant-Colonel C.C.I. Merritt won his Victoria Cross at Pourville. This picture was taken while he was a captain in his original regiment, the Seaforth Highlanders of Canada. [DND]

Despite a slight head wound caused by an exploding cannon shell and considerable damage to the rudder of his Spitfire, Flight Sergeant Mehew 'Zip' Zobell of Raymond, Alberta, flew his machine safely back to England. [DND]

And that was why Air Commodore Cole wanted an extra half-hour to ensure enough air cover for the evacuation.

The air support controller, who apparently knew nothing of the Army Co-operation Command system of Air Support Signals Units (ASSUs), would have liked at least two more squadrons at his beck and call in order to fulfil his functions properly; and, in his post-raid report, he complained of the lack of information reaching him. *'No signals were received by me from Uxbridge,'* he anguished, *'so that it was not known what targets had been accepted and what squadrons were on their way.'* Nor was he able to obtain current information from the beaches, noting that in his opinion, *'forward controllers needed to be close to the leading troops, where they could actually observe the flow of battle and talk directly to pilots over VHF radio.'*

All that had been incorporated in the Army Co-operation system, but:

...at Fighter Command, [Lieutenant-Colonel] Ralph Stockley [the army liaison officer] had not even been let into the [JUBILEE] secret, and his assistant at 11 Group, where Leigh-Mallory fought the air battle, had been 'frozen out.' There were no ALOs with the Fighter Squadrons who carried out low level attacks, and therefore no adequate briefing, no ASSU tentacles forward to the beaches and backwards to the airfields.

The end result was that impromptu air support was often delivered in the wrong places and was always too slow in arriving. A thoroughly frustrated Colonel Carrington, the army liaison officer at Bomber Command, prepared a critical analysis on 'the misuse of 2 Group in JUBILEE, the only corner of the muddle that [he] was entitled to speak upon with authority.' He continued:

I examined the close support attacks made by 2 Group bombers: the first attack missed a pre-arranged target by about two thousand yards; the second was indiscriminate bombing of a large area in which there might or might not have been Canadian troops; the third was not a suitable target.... The only useful thing 2 Group did that day was to lay smokescreens, and even those prevented the Headquarters ship from seeing what happened on the beaches.

The four aerial reconnaissance squadrons from Army Co-operation Command, including Nos 400 and 414 Squadrons, RCAF (flying North American Mustang Is with Allison engines that were nowhere near as effective a fighting instrument as later Mustang variants with Rolls-Royce powerplants) had been briefed to 'discover movements of enemy reinforcements towards the area in which our Army [was] operating.'

The likeliest routes were the main roads from Rouen, Le Havre and Amiens, and each of those was covered hourly by a pair of Mustangs. 'Although much negative information

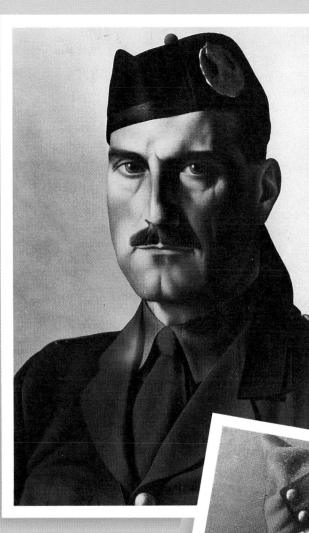

Major A.T. Law, Queen's Own Cameron Highlanders of Canada, 'successfully and efficiently fought his unit approximately two miles inland, inflicting heavy casualties on the enemy,' according to the citation for his DSO. [From an oil painting by Lawren Harris – National Gallery of Canada]

An older man, who had joined the militia in 1932, Lance-Sergeant G.A. Hickson, Royal Canadian Engineers, was awarded a Distinguished Service Medal for his 'determined leadership' at Dieppe and would subsequently win a Military Medal in North Africa, ending the war with the rank of captain. [From an oil painting by Lawren Harris – National Gallery of Canada]

was received, the only positive information was a report of three to five light tanks 10 miles south of Dieppe.' Whether they were actually there or not is a moot issue, but they certainly never came into action.

Lesser roads in the vicinity of the battlefield were patrolled with a regularity that after-action analysis suggested should be discouraged. 'Every half hour a pilot would fly up or down the same road, so that the [anti-aircraft] gun crews were ready for him. Although it is difficult to vary such tasks, irregular timing would help' — a blindingly obvious conclusion that no doubt owed something to the fact that ten reconnaisssance machines were lost during the day, only one of them being Canadian.

German aircraft, whether fighters, bombers or dive-bombers, were, by and large, not much interested in the ground battle. *'Throughout the day there was constant activity in the air,'* recalled Colonel Labatt of the RHLI, lying behind the sea wall on White Beach with his adjutant and signallers.

Following the initial machine-gunning of the 'front' by our fighters, German fighters and recce planes came over to see what it was all about. These were immediately engaged by our machines. Formations were broken up and individual planes started chasing each other all over the sky. Many were brought down, but at such a distance that we were unable to tell whether they were British or German.

Later, waves of light and medium bombers of the Luftwaffe roared over us at about 1,800 feet. Their objective was the boat pool established some three miles out. These were engaged by our fighters and the Flak ships guarding the pool. The attacks were pressed home by the Germans with great persistence and courage, for bomber after bomber was shot down, either going to pieces in the air or diving into the sea with a terrific crash, yet they kept coming in for more.

Their sticks of bombs exploded on the water or the boats with appalling detonations which we could hear and feel even above the noise on the beach. Pillars of water 300 feet high rose vertically as their bombs burst. It was spectacular.

As soon as von Rundstedt, *Oberbefehlshaber West*, learned that the raiders were showing signs of trying to evacuate the remnants of their force, he began exhorting his men *'to destroy what can be destroyed.... It is up to us now — and I am pressing this point — to wipe out just as many of the enemy as is in any way possible.... Every available weapon must now contribute to the complete destruction of the enemy.'*

With the Germans obediently striving to destroy whatever was left of the raiding force, whatever the weaknesses and shortcomings of the RAF in supporting the troops earlier, it did valuable work now. The USAAF B-17s, escorted by the four Spitfire IX

Making the best of a bad job, a prisoner uses one of his gaiters to keep the sun off his head. [ECP Armées]

Unhappy warriors. [ECP Armées]

This young soldier found that his steel helmet made a good drinking vessel. [ECP Armées]

These soldiers are beginning to cheer up, perhaps as they realize how lucky they are to have survived the battle. [ECP Armées]

The Canadian wounded were collected at a nearby convent before being shipped out to hospitals as far afield as Paris. [ECP Armées]

Their hands raised in surrender, dispirited Canadians trudge through the streets of Dieppe, nearly all of them towards two and a half years of prison camp life. [ECP Armées]

The man in the middle, without his trousers, may have been one of those who tried to swim to safety but had to turn back. He shows no sign of being wounded and may simply have been exhausted. [ECP Armées]

A wounded soldier is carried through the streets of Dieppe by two of his comrades and a helpful Frenchman. [ECP Armées]

Only two hundred more Canadians were taken prisoner in the eleven-month north-west Europe campaign, 1944-1945, than in the eleven-hour Dieppe raid, 1942. [NAC]

Generalleutnant *Konrad Haase, commander of the Dieppe defences and the 302nd Infanteriedivision (right), discusses the battle with a bemedalled young officer – holder of the Knight's Cross and German Cross in Gold – of 10* Panzerdivision. *The latter is possibly 24-year-old* Hauptmann *Georg Grüner, who had won his decorations on the Eastern Front in 1941 and would be killed in action there during the spring of 1944. [DND]*

A contingent of the Kriegsmarine *march through the streets of Dieppe on the way to bury their dead. [ECP Armées]*

German guards pose for the camera while Canadian prisoners – some in uniform, some in shirt sleeves, at least one wrapped in a blanket – wait to be marched off. [NAC]

A French civilian first-aid worker (wearing a Canadian steel helmet) and a bare-headed Canadian dress the leg wound of a British sailor. [ECP Armées]

A loaf of bread conveniently to hand on the wooden board he is using as a pillow, this wounded Canadian felt glad to be alive. [ECP Armées]

Another civilian first-aider watches over an injured Canadian captain alert enough to follow the photographer with his eyes, while a more seriously wounded RNVR lieutenant lies on a stretcher oblivious to events around him. [ECP Armées]

On the edge of the esplanade, four soldiers – one of them wounded – wait for German orders. The lance-corporal with his back to the camera has probably been using his steel helmet as a seawater receptacle to bathe the injured man's wounds. He is still wearing the helmet liner. [ECP Armées]

squadrons, bombed the enemy airfield at Abbeville and put its runways temporarily out of commission, thus substantially weakening the *Luftwaffe's* fighter effort, while nine squadrons of RAF/RCAF fighters gathered over the beaches to cover the withdrawal.

At Puys, there was no one left to be taken off, the survivors having surrendered at about 0830 hours. One LCA had managed to return to the beach, but *'no one appeared for some time'* according to evidence presented at the *Queen Emma* enquiry. *'Then there was a rush of soldiers from hiding to try and get into boat. There were heavy casualties during process'*, all to no purpose. The badly-overloaded craft was sunk by a bomb or shell a few yards offshore and among those killed was its gallant commander, Lieutenant E.R. Ramsay, RNVR.

On most of Red Beach nothing could reach the shore. One LCT was hit and exploded amidships while trying to do so, and the only Essex Scottish to escape were those who could reach the shelter of an abandoned LCT, close to the junction with White Beach, which also provided shelter for LCAs beaching on the far side of it. (Stapleton, who would surely have made it if anybody did, had been ordered by his commanding officer to look after the wounded and, being the good soldier that he was, he stayed with them to the end.)

On White Beach (where the chaplain of the RHLI, Honorary Captain J.W. Foote, was collecting and succouring the wounded in a style that would bring him a VC), discipline understandably began to break down as landing craft tried to sneak in under cover of a well-laid smokescreen — which rapidly drifted inland, leaving them exposed to ever more intense fire. Brigadier Southam noted that the appearance of the boats *'was the signal for a headlong rush of several hundred men who waded into the water, shoulder deep, in an attempt to board them.'* The gallant Sergeant Hickson also *'saw a great rush of infantry down from the centre of the beach towards the boats'*, but the surprising thing is not that there was so much panic — if that is the word — but that there was so little.

'At 1245 five A[ssault] L[anding] C[raft] appeared, making for the centre of White Beach,' reported the Royal Navy lieutenant in charge of the beach party there.

> *While coming in, two were put out of action by the enemy but the remaining three touched down on the beach. ...these were quickly loaded and had just shoved off when there was a rush of Military personnel towards the departing craft.... but the few extra men who had managed to scramble aboard, together with timely enemy fire, upset the trim of the craft and she sank. One of the remaining craft received a direct hit and sank, but the third managed to get away to sea.*

Most of those who tried simply could not 'get away to sea.' The experience of Labatt was typical and he recorded it in more detail than most from the relative tranquility of that German prison camp.

The beach was under direct fire from all arms at 250 yards and over. The day was sunny and the only cover for troops crossing the beach was light smoke from burning tanks, landing craft, bursting projectiles and the stranded vehicles themselves.

I was just wondering how many would survive the gauntlet when from the East appeared two Hurricanes flying at 200 feet along the water's edge. They laid the most perfect smokescreen I have ever seen from one end of the beach to the other.* They, of course, became the target for every German weapon within range, and I was delighted to see them disappear to the westward, apparently unscathed. It was a daring operation and I hope the pilots received full recognition for their act.

Under cover of the smoke, which drifted slowly inland, small groups began...to move towards the water. The first and largest was a crowd of German prisoners, carrying our wounded from the Casino, some using doors and other makeshifts as stretchers....

...After the smoke had come down and while it was thick, enemy firing

faded to almost nothing.... As the air cleared, however, fire became very much brisker....

There was no beach control. However, all the boats within our limited range of visibility were loaded and starting to turn. We moved to the East, to see how things were going there. Here the rear groups who had run across the beach were wading out to the A[ssault] L[anding]C[raft], waiting to get off shore. We did likewise and clambered into the last and most Easterly boat. It was frightfully crowded....

We were no sooner aboard than the smoke cleared completely, leaving us exposed right under the German guns.... In no time the sea was littered with the wreckage of shattered ALCs and dotted with heads and waving arms. A shell burst inside the crowded boat next to us with ghastly results.

I could feel our craft being hit but was not conscious of anything else until I saw the naval crew jump overboard and found that I was standing in water up to my knees.... I decided to swim out to a T[ank] L[anding] C[raft] half a mile offshore....

As I neared the TLC I realized that it was being shelled; and when about 200 yards from it, it received two direct hits...and began to settle by the stern. I couldn't believe my eyes.... However, when there was nothing to be seen but bows sticking vertically out of the water, I realized that she wasn't in very good shape. Neither was I.... As the only other craft in sight was miles

---

* A considerable number of men had already been captured — or compelled to surrender — before this smokescreen was laid.

Condensation trails of dog-fighting aircraft weave patterns in the flawless blue sky over Dieppe, 19 August 1942. [ECP Armées]

Major-General J.H. Roberts, DSO, MC, GOC 2nd Canadian Infantry Division, and Land Force commander at Dieppe. '...a fighting soldier who carried out the orders he was given and acted like a gentleman....' [From an oil painting by Lawren Harris – National Gallery of Canada]

German Flak gunners man their anti-aircraft gun during the battle. [DND]

away on the horizon, I turned reluctantly towards the shore.

The return trip was very trying. The tide had taken me a bit to the East and I landed behind a TLC stranded broadside high above the present water line. The fire had increased if anything and I was horrified by the number of dead washing upon the beach. Sheltering behind and lying around the TLC were 150-200 men of all units, nearly all wounded. They were in shocking condition and were being constantly sniped [at], machine-gunned and mortared.

I made a recce and decided to get all the wounded inside the TLC as it offered the best cover available. Coming out of the TLC, I met Bill Southam, who was trying to organize Brens [light machine-guns] and rifles to keep down close sniping.... He had been hit in the leg...

Several tanks were still firing, playing a major role both in holding the Germans back and suppressing at least some of their fire, but there was nothing more that could be done. *'The injuries were appalling and many could neither be shifted nor properly tended, yet I never heard one complaining — and if one cried out or groaned, he tried to apologise for it afterwards,'* remembered Southam. Among them was Ed Bennett, who had been severely injured hours earlier — before he had even landed, in fact — but who had fought his tank up and down the esplanade, and then again on the beach, until one track was smashed by a German shell.

At this moment a tank officer was led past. His whole face had been burnt off and both eyes were blinded. Probably permanently.* He must have been in agony, yet his spirit was magnificent. I heard him say, 'Remember, boys, if it comes, give only your name, rank and number.'

There could no longer be any question of 'if it comes.' It seems likely that a good many of the survivors had already surrendered and there was certainly nothing to be gained by further resistance. Labatt and those around him were probably the last to give up from Red and White beaches.

I quickly made the most unpleasant decision of my life. A captured German airman was with us. I warned the nearby tanks to cease fire and sent him out with a white towel. Never before had I seen such a pleased expression come over a man's face. He had had an exhilarating day. Firing died down, mortar shells ceased to fall, 30-40 Germans leaped up on the sea wall.... I looked at my watch. It was exactly 1500 hours.

Off Green Beach, at Pourville, the plywood R-boats that had brought the Camerons across the Channel had twice started for shore, only to be called back because of the heavy fire — to the heartfelt relief of Able Seaman Kirby, if not the men on the beach. Evacuating them was left to the

---

* Happily, Bennett only lost the sight of one eye permanently.

The chaplain of the Royal Hamilton Light Infantry, Honorary Captain J.W. Foote, won the Victoria Cross for his work with the wounded at Dieppe. [DND]

After the raid, the Germans demolished what was left of the Casino to improve their field of fire from the West Headland. [DND]

inadequately armoured (and too few) LCAs. *'The process of thinning out began about 1045 hours and at exactly 1104 hours the first LCAs appeared,'* according to Major Law.

As soon as the troops began to cross the beach, a very heavy cross fire from machine-guns and musketry came down upon them. There was also mortar fire and some shellfire.... A beach party had been organized by the S. Sask. R. and the troops went down to the beach as LCAs became available. Some enemy prisoners were used as stretcher-bearers and did the work very efficiently.

The Camerons completed their re-embarkation about 1200 hours, having suffered more heavily during this last phase of the withdrawal than during all the previous stages of the operation.

Luckily for him, Flight Sergeant Nissenthal was among those who got away, but Lieutenant Kempton of the Camerons' N⁰ 14 Platoon was not so fortunate, being *'hit when they opened fire on me,'* according to his devoted platoon sergeant. *'He... died instantly, as he would no doubt have wished to, protecting his men to the last.'*

Also busy protecting his men — but, happily, not to the last — was the South Saskatchewans' Colonel Merritt. The bridge that made him famous has since been named 'Merritt Bridge,' with a plaque on it to record the fact, but the beach itself might have been a more appropriate memorial.

The party left on the beach, which included Lt.-Col. Merritt, some of the officers of his Regt. and about six officers of the QOCH of C, withdrew to a relatively sheltered position behind the sea wall. From scaffolding that had been erected by workmen repairing the wall, they were able to bring fire on the enemy and keep them off from about 1100 hours until 1530 hours. During this time Capt. Runcie witnessed an act of exceptional gallantry performed by Lt.-Col. Merritt. He advanced alone across 300 yards of bullet-swept beach to bring in a wounded corporal lying at the water's edge. At 1530 hours Lt-Col Merritt called a council of the surviving officers, and it was decided that as enemy strength was increasing all the time, and it was no longer possible to inflict casualties, further resistance was useless.

Colonel Catto's little party of Royals would lurk in their copse behind the East Headland for another hour before surrendering; but except for them, Merritt's group were the last to hoist the white flag. JUBILEE was over.

'A great many questions kept running through my mind as we ploughed our way through the waters of the English Channel, retracing the course that we had spent all last night following to France, remembered Able Seaman Kirby. *'At any moment we expected to be attacked by Stuka dive bombers or Junkers 88s as our boats staggered, hodge-podge, towards Blighty.'*

A few hours earlier, these tired, beaten men had been expecting to walk the streets of Dieppe as conquering heroes. What a pity that Mountbatten, Hughes-Hallett, McNaughton and Crerar did not go ashore! [ECP Armées]

Canadian prisoners – one barefooted – stumble down a street lined with watchful German soldiers. [ECP Armées]

One of the two concrete bunkers that guarded the seaward side of the Casino. This damage may have been done by a 4-inch shell but more likely marks the beginning of the process of demolishing the entire Casino, as the Germans did after the Raid. [ECP Armées]

The *Luftwaffe* was interested in bigger things than Kirby's R-boat. Flight Lieutenant D.R. Morrison of 401 Squadron had been brought down by debris from a German bomber he had destroyed, and he was then picked out of the water by an air/sea rescue launch.

We saw an attack by German bombers on the returning convoy beaten back by heavy ack-ack [anti-aircraft] fire from the ships. We saw the explosion and pall of black smoke caused by two Spitfires colliding head-on. We watched gunfire fom the shore batteries being returned by the ships and saw some Bostons and also destroyers laying smokescreens to protect the convoys.

Later in the afternoon, in company with two other rescue launches, they were attacked by FW 190s. The other vessels were set on fire.

Our launch was not damaged too badly but our radio was knocked out. We pulled over and...started to pick up the survivors from the two furiously burning launches. Their fuel and ammunition was exploding and many of the men in the warm water were screaming with pain... We picked up fourteen survivors and the Navy boat picked up four — there should have been twenty-two! [...]

Since the survivors were so badly wounded, the skipper raced back to Newhaven at full throttle... Up until that time we had no idea of how things had gone for the troops. We soon found out that they had taken a terrible beating.

As for the navy, the destroyer *Berkeley* had been so badly damaged that she had to be sunk by 'friendly fire,' and *Brocklesby, Fernie* and *Calpe* were each hit. So were a number of other vessels, mostly landing craft, large and small — 33 of them being lost, altogether.

Kirby was back in England before dark, no doubt wondering in the back of his mind if the decision to sell his week-end pass had been a wise one. There were other emotions.

The sun was resting on the horizon when we finally caught sight of dear old England. What a wonderful sight to see... What a mixture of feeling went through my body as I climbed up to the jetty and surveyed the shambles throughout the harbour. So relieved to be home. So happy to be in one piece. So ashamed to have come home alone. So proud of the way the Camerons went to their deaths. So sad that they seemed to have been wasted. So angry that I was even a part of something so confusing, agonizing, demanding, and apparently unrewarding, without even knowing what I was doing or exactly where I had been.

CONCLUSION

CONCLUSION

The original plan for the raid on Dieppe — Operation RUTTER — was gravely flawed, to such an extent that it should have been obvious to any concerned professional at the time.

The plan for JUBILEE — a *'bull-necked plan,'* Lord Lovat called it — was worse. Thus it was that, in human terms, German casualties — killed, wounded, taken prisoner and missing — numbered only 591 (army 316, navy 113, and air force 162), while Anglo-Canadian losses totalled 4,350 (army 3,610 — including 247 of the 1,057 commandos and Rangers, navy 550, and air force 190).

Mountbatten and his acolyte, Hughes-Hallet, could hardly avoid taking some of the blame. They spent the rest of their lives, however, endeavouring to avoid taking more of it; but, cleverly, they made no attempt to shift it on to others, a technique which might well have led to mutual mudslinging.

Damage control was everything, and every time a critical letter appeared in the Press, anywhere in the world, or a harsh word about them was uttered on radio — or, later, on television — they were quick to respond. The Mountbatten archives must be full of correspondence between that gruesome twosome, and with others, discussing how one accusation or another might be sidestepped or refuted. Yet, as the years passed and historians dug deeper into once-closed archives, it became harder and harder for them to do so. Lord Lovat, who was as well qualified to speak on the subject as any man alive, wrote (in 1965):

> *Hard things were said after the raid but the top brass survived the post-mortem by finding a convenient scapegoat in the person of Gen[eral] Hamilton Roberts...a fighting soldier who carried out the orders he was given and acted like a gentleman in accepting his dismissal [shortly afterwards] in silence without protest.*

The brass that condemned Roberts was Canadian, not British.

Earlier raids — even earlier raids planned largely under Mountbatten's *aegis*, such as the Vaagsö affair — had gone off well enough. But prior to the St. Nazaire raid, planning had largely been in the hands of the men, like Lovat, who would have to carry out those plans; only intelligence and co-ordinating functions were handled by COHQ, which, under the direction of Admiral Keyes, had never numbered more than

DIEPPE, DIEPPE

149

two dozen people altogether, including secretaries!

Then came Mountbatten as he was in the spring of 1942, a man whom the one-time regular officer, novelist and wartime commando, Major Robert Henriques (he had been Haydon's chief of staff at Vaagsö), described perfectly in his posthumously published *From a Biography of Myself:*

>*...the only weak feature of this most genuine of War Lords — the not small, but smallish eyes, too close together by only a fraction — was inevident; and the face represented for Meego all that he would always covet of power, personality and assurance; and ambition justified; a vast ambition that was not reprehensible, because it exactly coincided with public interest; an imperial ambition, superbly equipped for any conquest, armed with a quick logical mind and an even swifter intuition; with no weakness except a total inability to judge men correctly, whether they were his cronies or his subordinates.*

Mountbatten's cronies and subordinates at Richmond Terrace numbered in the hundreds, and we have seen what a fighting soldier such as Lovat thought of them. But, inevitably, as raids got larger more planners were needed, and it became necessary that COHQ play a greater role in the planning process.

The results were not promising. At St. Nazaire the primary objective had been attained only because a large degree of surprise had been achieved; but surprise, where a competent enemy is concerned, is almost always partly a matter of luck and, by definition, cannot last long. Casualties at St. Nazaire had been extraordinarily heavy, and none of the secondary objectives had been attained, but because the destruction of the drydock was of such strategic importance the operation could be accounted a success.

In RUTTER, those called upon to carry out the weight of the raid — by their own leaders, we must remember — lacked either the knowledge or the confidence (perhaps both) to criticize the Outline Plan handed to them. Roberts' and Mann's detailed planning was no better than that of COHQ; and for reasons we may never know, those people in Home Forces (particularly Montgomery) who might have put them on the right track chose not to do so.

The plan that resulted was overly complex, requiring precisely integrated timing, the execution of each part of it dependent upon the perfect execution of the previous part. Comprehension of the enemy's defences was quite inadequate, there was no appreciation of the inevitable 'friction of war' (not to mention the 'fog'), and fire support was far too slight. When surprise was lost, all would be lost.

The question of lack of formal authorization for JUBILEE — which

By the time this picture was taken, in 1952, John Hughes-Hallett (standing, right) had risen to the rank of rear-admiral. Standing on the left, Crown Prince Olaf of Norway. Seated, left to right, Admiral Sir Patrick Brind, H.M. King Haakon of Norway, Admiral Sir George Creasey. [IWM]

Bound together by recollections of shared danger, as well as by their arms about each other's shoulders, two soldiers of Les Fusiliers Mont-Royal who escaped unharmed pose for a picture a week after the raid. [NAC]

Villa has proven circumstantially beyond a reasonable doubt, however unlikely it may seem — is the really interesting one. Winston Churchill and the British chiefs of staff desperately needed some major operation in north-west Europe, and they all knew very well what Mountbatten was doing. Why, then, did they not make sure that it had every possible chance of success, putting all their formal and informal weight into ensuring that it would be so?

There is, even today, no clear answer to that question, but the likeliest one is that their need was too urgent. To put all of JUBILEE's faults right would have taken more time than they could afford, so that they preferred to let it run its course, imperfect though they knew it to be. Leaving everything to Mountbatten, they simply hoped for the best. In doing so, of course, they created the conditions to make a bad situation worse.

JUBILEE was worse, for it had all the faults of RUTTER exaggerated and compressed into an even tighter timetable. With Baillie-Grohman gone, the chiefs of staff, Home Forces and most of COHQ's few experienced planners virtually 'out of the loop,' the RAF little interested in the ground battle and the prime minister anxious to placate his Russian ally, Hughes-Hallett was left with a free hand. And it would seem that he was obsessed by the need to put through JUBILEE.

So, apparently, were Generals McNaughton and Crerar, who failed badly in not casting more critical eyes on his planning. Indeed, Mountbatten's wise decision (from his perspective) not to cast any stones meant that they were not even bruised, although their responsibility for the JUBILEE disaster was as clear as anybody's; although they made — so far as we can tell — no serious effort to fulfil it, leaving everything to Mountbatten above them and Roberts below.

Perhaps too much of their concern was focussed on the Canadian politics that lay athwart the issue, but the last word could well lie with Admiral Sir Bertram Ramsay, who knew a good deal about amphibious operations, having supervised the evacuation from Dunkirk in June 1940 and the return to Normandy exactly four years later. 'Dieppe was a tragedy,' he thought, 'and the cause may be attributed to the fact that it was planned by inexperienced enthusiasts.'

Were the lessons of JUBILEE vital to the success of OVERLORD two years later, as was subsequently claimed by Mountbatten (for the first time at a chiefs of staff meeting the day after the raid); and since then by many veterans seeking consolation for what happened to them and their comrades ?

Well, a case can certainly be made that those same lessons could have been learned at far less cost through a combination of common sense,

Men who were not there sympathize with some of those who were. The bare-headed men in the centre and on the right still showed signs of the strain they had undergone, when this picture was taken, four days later. [NAC]

After the liberation of Dieppe in August 1944, officers and men of the Royal Hamilton Light Infantry pause to offer a prayer over the graves of some of their comrades who were killed there two years earlier. [NAC]

forethought, and hard work. Taking a port without having it seriously damaged was a most unlikely scenario, for example, a possibility which should have been dismissed out of hand; and long-range planners were already toying with techniques of landing and supplying large forces over open beaches — and with the idea of artificial harbours.

The First World War should have taught every thoughtful soldier — and certainly every soldier who had fought in it — that a set-piece frontal assault without total surprise or overwhelming fire support was suicidal; although, on the evidence of Dieppe, both McNaughton and Crerar (First World War gunners with a wealth of staff experience in that conflict) apparently had learned nothing. Effective command and control required that communications not be of the makeshift variety employed aboard *Calpe* and *Fernie*. The same had been true of First World War gunnery and two 'old hands' such as McNaughton and Crerar should have known that, too, and been alert to the danger.

The only lessons that needed to be learned the hard way were essentially those of scale — the larger the operation, the more likely the unforeseeable to occur and the more difficult to guarantee success. Even those could be practised in exercises, however, and all the lessons needed for D-Day but unobtainable through training and foresight were to be learned from the vastly greater and more complex landings in north-west Africa (8 November 1942), Sicily (9-10 July 1943), Salerno (9 September 1943), and even Anzio (22 January 1944).

There remains the question of setting well-trained but totally inexperienced troops to carry out what was generally recognised as the most difficult operation of war — establishing a foothold on a hostile shore. The German assessment was blunt and to the point — *'English* [i.e., commandos] *fought well. Canadians and Americans not so well, later quickly surrendered under the impression* [sic] *of the high, bloody losses.'*

Marking the fiftieth anniversary of Dieppe in the journal *History Today*, one-time British official historian M.R.D. Foot observed that '2 Canadian Division had never been under fire before, with an unhappy result. The first thing many soldiers did on being shot at was to lie down. Having once lain down, they were disinclined to get up again; one of the reasons for the raid's failure.'

He touched a raw nerve with many patriotic Canadians, who saw in his words an imputation of cowardice and resented them accordingly. His point — likely shared by von Rundstedt — was one of inadequate tactical training and inexperience, however, not of heroism or cowardice. The 2nd Division, like every other division in every other army, contained its share of cowards as well as heroes and, no doubt, a number of the former were among those who lay down.

Many potentially brave men, stunned by the noise and violence of battle, also lay down or held back, not knowing what else to do, but Foot was surely wrong to attribute the raid's failure to their response. Had every man there been a Hector or Achilles, a battle as poorly planned and organized as JUBILEE would have been very hard to win: only gross German incompetence could have made it otherwise.

TABLE OF CONTENTS